ALL RITES REVERSED?!

Ritual Technology for Self-Initiation

by
Antero Alli
& Guests

Introduced by
Robert Anton Wilson

1988
FALCON PRESS
PHOENIX, ARIZONA 85012, U.S.A.

ISBN: 0-941404-81-1
Library of Congress Card Catalog Number: 87-50537
Copyright Registration Number: TX 2-008-582

OTHER TITLES BY THE AUTHOR
ANGEL TECH: *A Modern Shaman's Guide to Reality Selection*
THE AKASHIC RECORD PLAYER: *A Non-Stop Geomantic Romance*
CHAPEL PERILOUS: *Dreaming Phases For Lovers* (stage play)
AS THE WORM TURNS: *A Psychic Soap Opera* (radio play)
ASTRO*TURF: *Down-To-Earth Astrology*
THE 21st CENTURY TAROT

PhotoMontages in this book by Antero
Occasional Art by Christi
Typesetting: MacIntosh Font: Laser Palatino
Cover Art ©1988 Wolfgang Gersch, METAART STUDIO
1115 32nd Street, Oakland, CA 94608, 415-652-2210
Layout Design by Antero

Limited First Edition — 1986
Second Revised Edition — 1987
VIGILANTERO PRESS
P.O. Box 7513 Boulder CO 80306

First Falcon Press Edition — 1988
FALCON PRESS
3660 N. 3rd St.
Phoenix, Arizona 85012
(602) 246-3546

Manufactured in the United States of America

ACKNOWLEDGEMENTS

The section of ALL RITES REVERSED dedicating itself to ***ritual theatre*** *emerged as a ten-year personal response to certain key principles introduced by David Rosenbloom during the Spring of 1976 in Berkeley, California. The keys of NO-FORM, CONTACT POINT and POLARIZATIONS were presented by David to a handful of participants experimenting with accessing spiritual sources in the body, primarily for self-knowledge. If it wasn't for David's inspired and deliberate role as initiator to these principles, the current medium of ritual theatre may never have come to pass. Thank you, David, wherever you are...*

Throughout the history of this medium of ritual theatre, other key individuals indirectly and/or directly shaped its destiny and they are:

JERZY GROTOWSKI...for his pioneering work & brilliant blue light
ANTONIN ARTAUD...for burning his tragic flaws so brightly
WILLIAM BLAKE...for so vividly envisioning the archetypes we all met
CHRISTOPHER S. HYATT...for the initiations and your menacing clarity
CARL C. JUNG...for his seminal literature on alchemical process
CHAMBER THEATRE TROUPE ...for your dilligence, grace,& the eternal
JANE BROWN...for engaging the values of relaxation, form and gravity
KEITH BERGER...for your early training, a lasting friendship & the future
SIMA WOLF...for fusing her sparkling, broken ballerina into the medium
ROBERT GREENWAY...for the invitation to legitimatize this work
NANCY LUNNEY/ESALEN...for bringing ritual theatre to Esalen
JOSE ARGUELLES...for waking up in a Mayan temple & living to tell it
G. GURDJIEFF...for the presence he instilled in the words that he spoke
URSA MAJOR (Allegra, Jim & John)...for our experimental designs

May this space express my deepest gratitude to

NO-FORM

CONTENTS

Guests of Honor

For Kallista
the Brightest Star in the Blackest Sky
&
To Christi
for her Severity of Devotion

PREFACE

By Robert Anton Wilson

Theatre is, and has always been, magic. The very word tragedy comes from tragos, goat-song, and refers to the ancient rituals in which the goat-god was sacrificed as an offering to the Earth Mother. Satire comes from satyr, the goat-man-god. Comedy, similarly, derives from comodo, a festival to ensure the fertility of the tribe. Indeed, the difference between drama and ritual depends almost entirely on what the audience is told on the way in to the scene of the action. Move a Solemn High Mass into the Ethel Barrymore Theatre, tell everybody it is an experimental, and they will experience it as theatre. Stage Waiting For Godot in a cathedral on Maundy Thursday, and it will function as a totally acceptable sacrament; and nobody will have any doubts about who Godot is.

Ibsen's Doll's House is allegedly the classic example of the "naturalistic" play -- the social drama, the "slice of life", from which all the ritual elements have been removed. Yet Nora's awakening is the same theme as that of the awakening in the Eleusinian Mysteries in ancient Athens, and when she slams the door the the resonance in the collective psyche is identical with that experience when the Bible is slammed on the pulpit and the candles extinguished on Maundy Thursday. The ritual of awakening is always a path through psychic death to psychic rebirth, and that happens as much to Nora as to any character in the more obviously ritualized dramas of Sophocles.

The new form of Ritual Theatre developed by Antero Alli in the past ten years is uniquely a product of our eclectic and revolutionary age. It is very, very old and very, very new. As Osiris says in the Egyptian Book of the Dead, "I am yesterday, today and the brother of tomorrow." To enter Antero Alli's magic circle is to experience that kind of time-warp: you become one with with the first paleolithic shamans dancing to the bear-god, you will know yourself **here now** as you have never known yourself before, and you plunge into science-fiction futures in which humanity is expanded mentally and physically beyond our wildest hopes. Meanwhile, everybody in and out of the theatre can enjoy it and use it right now.

ROBERT ANTON WILSON, Ph.D.
INSTITUTE FOR THE STUDY OF THE HUMAN FUTURE
Author of *COSMIC TRIGGER, MASKS OF THE ILLUMINATI, THE NEW INQUISITION, SEX & DRUGS, PROMETHEUS RISING, & others*

INTENT

This book presents the development and internal workings of a ritual technology dedicated to the process of Self-Initiation. This particular medium came about over a ten-year period of working alone and in conjunction with a multitude of groups from many walks of life. For the most part, it has served as a tool for self-knowledge although occasionally, with the right group, it's been elevated to *performance ritual.* For lack of better terms, I've chosen to call this medium **ritual theatre** . Ritual theatre combines elements from both ritual and theatre, as if it were rooted in the former and branching out into the latter. It is primarily a **non-performance** medium complete unto itself yet has proven effective for enhancing any ceremonial tasks, including preparation for live theatre.

Ritual, and its purpose, is refered to hereafter by those activities triggering awareness of our living relationship with the entity embodied *as this planet.* We are, as human beings, indigenous to this planet. Ritual serves to enhance our unique placement...who we are and why we are here. As Global Inhabitants, we are here to participate with the planetary entity in a certain way. At the root, we are feeding off the Earth and it is feeding off of us. As we become more aware of this underlying reality, Planetary Intelligence can be said to be awakening within us. Earth Renewal Rites are those intentional activities serving the specific function of feeding the planetary entity. Human Renewal Rites are those which help us draw power, support and instruction from planetary energies. There is a reciprocal feeding occuring and ritual tunes us into its innate patterns.

DNA, as we know, is the genetic blueprint of life. Its complex, mandalic code interconnects all living forms in a planetary communications system of which every member/creature/being has a direct line to. DNA is also the native language of the planetary entity. When human beings learn how to **resonate** with and think like DNA, we'll have the distinct privilege of being listed in the Planetary Directory. Like the Aboriginies and their Dreamtime, A.T. & T. will be replaced by resonant telepathy. How a "human resonator" is developed is a primary ritualistic concern. As DNA instructs RNA Messenger molecule how to manufacture protein for its sustenance, so does the planetary entity instruct human beings in the task of feeding itself. To become receptive to this information, we have only to surrender to the Earth and become conduits for its transmission.

The overall purpose of ritual theatre is with the internal construction of a resonator. Resonance develops through the accumulation and integration of certain essences innate to one's being. Ritual theatre work triggers innate patterns of motion and being for the purpose of their assimilation.

The development of resonance depends on a certain willingness to sacrifice those icons, dogmas, and ideations no longer coinciding with the innate. Personal growth is excited with those encounters revealing conflict and/or struggle between **what we have learned** and **any real friction produced while relating to the innate.** The friction of this conflict has a way of feeding the innate being within us by cultivating the disconcerting awareness of **our need to transform and mutate.** A human resonator builds itself through the direct-knowledge of these four interdependent centers/selves/realities: PHYSICAL - EMOTIONAL - CONCEPTUAL - SOCIAL / SPIRITUAL. In essence, we are not human beings having a spiritual experience but spiritual beings having a human one. In this way, we share spiritual resonance with the planetary entity.

After developing a strong internal resonator, it is possible to enter the realm of performance ritual. To the degree we are in true resonance with certain essential forces, within and around us, is the degree we are moved and animated by these. Whatever essence authentically moves us, **also moves others.** The particular type of performance refered to here is ritualistic in nature as it seeks to invoke and preserve certain primordial qualities over the sophisticated theatrical persona. Consider it a primitive "sacred theatre" placing interpersonal interaction secondary to an *interplay of forces* which use the performers as their mode of expression. This kind of performance ceremony provokes the possibility of performers and audience to partake in spiritual communion or, holiness. The kind of performer required to incite this type of miracle is unique and talented. For the most part, his/her personality has become flexible (polarized) enough for an "innate synchronization" to occur...one serving the purpose of direct spiritual transmission.

Humans are ritualistic creatures and innately know more about how rituals work than one might suspect. My dream was to present this material in a way to actively enhance whatever ritual technology or ceremonial task is already engaging you, the reader, and perhaps, help dislodge hereto unknown techniques and insights imbedded deep inside your instincts. The challenge of writing *ALL RITES REVERSED* was in not getting a-head of myself but letting my **knowledge develop simultaneously with my being.** I could've only written this book **after** doing this stuff for about ten years first. This is how any kind of real understanding has come to pass, I think. In researching this book, I realized the limitations of my personal knowledge early on and so, invited several guest writers to describe their process of "preparing for, designing and executing effective ritual." Certain key individuals were also interviewed by myself to infuse the book with their immediate and valuable responses. These guests reside in the final section of this book, as if gathered there for a culminating ceremony.

Ritual theatre is a LAB for testing the simultaneous growth of our knowledge and being; it is a reality check to our understanding & ...reality checks never bounce. (Read *UNDOING YOURSELF* by C.S. Hyatt; Falcon Press) . To support self-exposure, this medium is presented as a "generic" ritual technology...one stripped of religious dogmas and imposed belief systems. (The author confesses the attempt to eliminate dogma as being a doctrine unto itself.) One of the overall objectives of a generic ritual technology is the excitation of ones own cosmologies into conscious recognition. We find out***what we are living for, what our lives revolve around and what we are feeding off of (and what feeds off us.)*** Of special interest is the discovery of what I call "the bones of ritual" or those ritual techniques common to many traditions. Each bone fits as a piece of a dancing skeleton...a ritual medium unfettered by cultural bias and/or brand-name, religious affiliation. This type of ritual technology is an open doorway to our direct-knowledge of the Infinite. Unearthing such magickal methodologies is an ongoing research for those psychic archeologists who have discovered enough relics to keep looking.

This ritual medium is not a particularly glamorous one. Quite frankly, its vigorous demands and zen-like starkness tend to turn some people right off. When there's a lot of "deep work" to do, the time alloted for personality worship is, or ought to be, dangerously slim. Once this is obvious, those attached to their emotional needs for personal recognition start complaining and/or realign with a different reason for being there. For those participating, this approach is set up to evoke Source Relations or encounter and dialog between Personality and Essence...Ego and Self...Illusion and Reality. The kind of conflict and internal pressure often resulting can be disconcerting to those just seeking personal gratification. However, for those willing to risk self-exposure and disillusionment, they see how conflict serves human development and *the birth of a soul.*

A central strand in this weave is learning perseverance to ones own subjective truth. With enough committment, a self-penetration occurs and we are allowed to braid ourselves into the collective fabric without losing our individual color. Coming from a highly "theatrical" background, I was very reluctant to surrender completely to my subjective experience for fear of exposing an "indulgent performance" which was, to my Actor's mentality, a fate worse than death. How was I to know that total committment to the Subjective eventually catalyzed a more objective awareness? I literally went kicking and screaming. The last thing I was going to let go of was the finely crafted sword of my will. I recall stages of being utterly lost in the sauce of my own preconceptions and losing sight of everything beyond my nose. Then there was that god-awful Dark Night of the Soul where King Confusion held court and my Foolish Intellect insisted on figuring it all out. (See DANGERS: Chapel Perilous).

After ten-plus years and thousands of rituals later, it seems I'm approaching Beginner's status. I know less now than I ever did before yet the work has allowed me to begin living my life. One thing is certain as I look back and that's this: Once you're ushered into The Magic Theatre of Self there's **no turning back.** As fellow visionary William Blake once remarked, "A fool who persists in his folly becomes wise." I might add that not only is Persistence a key...Surrender is the lock...Transformation the doorway and Being, the way out. Ritual theatre tends to be *psychotherapeutic* as it brings to light those repressed and hidden aspects of ourselves. This is, however, **not** psycho-drama, gestalt nor encounter group format. Herein is a complete medium unto itself, its integrity maintained by the understanding and practice of certain guidelines called Ritual Functions, the backbone of this technology.

This book is called ALL RITES REVERSED for various reasons, one of which is that its approach to ritual-design runs contrary to most others by the virtue of its emphasis on *solitude*. When a group meets to work in this medium, they prepare alone for as much as two hours before interacting. This is a device for cultivating the creative tension and individual integrity required to ignite spontaneous offering relatively unbiased by social obligations and insecurities. This orientation develops from the individual first before collective interplay and even then, solitude is sustained by each individual's contact with their **internal dependence** or, Source. This book is an appendige to actual work. Bring it with you when entering your magic circle. Show it to people suffering from ritual expertise. Use the book until your own ritual yoga develops and then, as a test, give the book away. Until then, you have my heartfelt permission to ***die and be reborn.*** *Ominos, Dominoes, Ear Nose and Eyes Know...Nobody Knows...*

Antero Alli
May Day 1987
Boulder COLORADO USA

ALL RITES REVERSED ?!

Ritual Technology for Self-Initiation

"Magicians, especially since the Gnostic and Quabala influences, have sought higher consciousness through the assimilation and control of universal opposites -- good/evil, positive/negative, male/female, etc. But due to the steadfast pomposity of ritualism inherited from the ancient methods of the shaman, occultists have been blinded to what is perhaps the two most important pairs of apparent or earth-plane opposites: ORDER/DISORDER *and* SERIOUS/HUMOROUS*. Magicians, and their progeny the scientists, have always taken themselves and their subject in a orderly and sober manner, thereby disregarding an essential metaphysical balance. When magicians learn to approach philosophy as a malleable art instead of an immutable Truth, and learn to appreciate the absurdity of man's endeavors, then they will be able to pursue their art with a lighter heart, and perhaps gain a clearer understanding of it, and therefore gain more effective magic.* ***CHAOS IS ENERGY."***

excerpted from **PRINCIPIA DISCORDIA**
by Greg Hill -- Loompanics Press

THE FIRST RITUAL

Principles of Ritual Theatre

One origin of the word ritual stems from *"root."* As a culture's traditions help maintain its identity and heritage, so do its rituals sustain the traditions themselves. Initially, a culture would develop around rituals not only to bring people together but to honor and preserve what was sacred and holy to **the land itself.** From a "geomantic" or Earth-based view, cultures are **geologically formed entities** determined by the topography of their particular planetary location. Thus, Tibetian Buddhist culture is indigenous and characteristic of the Himalyas, as are the Yaqui Indian traditions innate to the Sonora deserts of Mexico. It is the Earth itself which forms culture by its reciprocal interaction with the humans inhabiting its surface. In this sense, **the Earth evolves us** and our rituals, the articulation of **its** evolution **through us.** (See GEOMANCY)

Ritual develops with human response to signals received from the living planetary entity (hereafter called GAIA). Ritual distinguishes itself from "routine" in that the former serves to enhance awareness of Self/World, whereas the latter functions to diminish it. Conscious interaction with GAIA awakens Global or Mythic Intelligence within us (See 7th Grade in *ANGEL TECH* by the author). The function of Global Intelligence is **mutation** through cultural transformation. This change initiates itself when an individual becomes a crucible for the evolution of new forms and traditions. Near the genesis of a culture, "originating rituals" emerge as **individual human response to GAIA** and, through bridging these to a collective, a basis for a Group Mind is formed. These originating, first rituals temper the bonding responsible for distinct cultures to evolve. It is in the spirit of this First Ritual that this text dedicates itself to and why this book is subtitled: Ritual Technology for Self-Initiation.

For the greater part, ritual knowledge from World Cultures has been reserved and coveted by some form of Church/State/Order as a methodology for social control. This is why traditional religions have only one pope and/or an elite corps of archbishops, abbotts and assorted exalted clergy. To this day, there remains only one priest to a congregation who claims the authority for executing the ritual functions of sanctification, benediction, communion, Etc.. This individual, who is usually a man, acts as the Mouthpiece To & From God and serves as a Middle Man between Congregation and their Source. This dynamic sets up an immediate heirarchy diminishing the Congregation's autonomous relations with Source. How can this heirarchy, that jams direct Source Relations, be bypassed ?

Let it be known that every Man, Woman and Child reading these lines is hereby officially proclaimed a Pope and/or High Priestess by the Highest Authority now available: You!

A fundamental knowledge of how rituals work sets us free to access our own Source Relations, without having to conform to externally-based doctrines of the religious or philosophical kind. Exploring ritual without buying into imposed dogmas invites a certain willingness to govern oneself. This type of self-dominion forms the basis for individual integrity, without which true group unity could never emerge. A unique group dynamic activates with the fullfillment of each individual's personal style of expression. This type of collective identity communicates a fierce quality of***Being*** shared equally amongst participating members. All are equal by the virtue that each member is responsible for being him/herself.

No matter what your spiritual orientation, there are certain ritual techniques common to, and pre-dating, all traditions which can greatly enhance whatever ceremony you're engaged in. These are "generic" ritual forms and they belong to nobody and everybody. Many of these are imbedded deep inside our innate, instinctual nature waiting to be dislodged into consciousness and put to work. There's a ganglia in the center of our brains (the "R-Complex") governing home-site selection forming the basis for several ritual functions, one being the task of **locating a setting** to execute ceremony in. Related to this instinct is our natural talent for **making a house *a home*** by Sanctifying its space thus, initiating a Rare Area conducive to sacred activity. In addition, our ability to **take dominion over a space** for specific ritual purposes is a direct expression of our territorial drives. Our mechanical tendency to project and assume meaning onto an otherwise Deep & Meaningless Universe is inherently the primitive phase of a very powerful ritual technique: **Conscious Projection...** the ability to intentionally **energize** an area outside of ones body with **"charge"** thus, **motivating a ritual.**

An essential function of ritual is in giving form to the innate so as to restore our contact with spiritual sources in the body. In this way,***ritual is the formalization of instinct.*** Ritual provides an outlet for the ongoing Marriage between Spirit and Body, and their offspring the Soul. Ceremony inherently activates culture within the individual, as tradition is maintained by its extension to others. Those cultures which understood the value of ***potentia*** or "the zero" (like the Mayans), were able to initiate an ongoing **intimacy with The Void.** This rather crucial ritual technique enables us to enter transformative process far more intentionally than ever before. Potentia, hereafter refered to as **NO-FORM**, is coaxed by our comfort **in not doing anything and/or being anybody.** No-Form is that part of us existing constantly in a potential state in that it has not become anything yet. No-Form does not have to be a goal or some kind of "spiritual arrival" (as some religions would have us believe) but a highly practical, multi-purpose tool for **dissolving** our identification with the forces of one ritual so we may begin another, **anew.** When each ritual is **begun and concluded in No-Form,** its central contents may develop authentically without the imposition of the contrived intentions that make so many other ritual technologies but empty, rote routines. (Read *ZEN MIND, BEGINNER's MIND* by Suzuki for NO-FORM Meditations)

In the initial training phase of a generic ritual technology, the forces evoked in ceremony are all drawn from Oneself... what Carl G. Jung calls "aspects of The Self...that unified, self-organizing entity we are all expressions of." Ritual, in this sense, is a Theatre of Self as it works to access the autonomous, universal forces animating our internal landscape with aspects like: Masculine/Feminine, The Four Elements, Order and Chaos, Creative/Destructive/Nourishing, The Anima and The Animus, Sleep-Dream-Awakening, Colors, Death/Rebirth, and a cast of thousands. Each individual expresses these universal aspects **in their own way,** yet we are all connected to them through our **Source Relations.** By locating our **contact points** with these living forces within, we develop a *resonating capacity* and the empathy so necessary for reading and responding to living signals from sources beyond our imagination, like...other people and the planet, for example. Internal resonance, then, lays the foundation for The First Ritual in its willingness **to look within.**

Like the archeologist's pick-axe, effective ritual is a tool for penetrating the surface crust of our social persona for treasures imbedded deep within our essential nature. This INITIATION process has traditionally engaged some form of **sense-deprivation.** A complete withdrawal of ones energy, attention and identification with the immediate environment is a necessary prerequisite for going within. As we gather our forces in this way, we mark the transition from *external* to **internal dependence.** When working with others, this means realizing your **non-responsibility** to them, socially speaking, so more internal freedom can be explored and established.

Ritual work tends to evoke a dynamic relationship between a person and their Source...personality and essence. One way of supporting this interaction is encouraging an "asocial" climate wherein participants bypass socialization and instead, **stabilize** their internal dependence. The release of social obligations sets up a kind of **Rare Area** conducive to asocial activities. A kind of interaction eventually develops as each participant accumulates enough *personal power* to have something meaningful to share. Source relations can be clarified by searching for what is truly *sacred.* The sacred implies, among other things, *what one lives for* or perhaps...ones Point of Worship (POW)...that area catalyzing revolution in our lives by the virtue of our lives revolving around it. Often times, the POW is unknown and, at best, obscure and shifting in and out of focus. The POW appears to reveal itself in our greatest **excitements and resistances**...areas of powerful **positive** and **negative emotional charge.** Ritual tends to unveil these hot spots for the purpose of self-knowledge, personal growth and, if they are accepted, ***self-transcendence.***

The perpetually renewing cycles of Nature demonstrates evolutionary process in the following manner. Fertile ground permiting, when a seed is planted... it sprouts from the Earth and grows, in time, to a tree. This tree blossoms and bears fruit which ripens and then drops to the ground where it breaks open, rots and goes to seed...offering the essential fecundity for the growth of a new tree. We might ask, **"What are the necessary conditions for conscious human evolution ?"** As we are outgrowths of Nature, we have locked away in the cellular memory of our bodies everything we need to know about transformative process. This information can be triggered and released throughout the fulfillment of the Body's most central need: **TO BE FELT DEEPLY**. This is why all "primitive" or Earth-based cultures instigate ritual preparation with some kind of physical and emotional warm-up. This time is dedicated to tuning the human instrument so we might become more willing to be played by the universal forces governing existence...what Carl Jung coined as The Archetypes. (Only when the instrument is tuned can it play **music.**)

In the ritual medium described and outlined hereafter, there is a 40-60 minute physical prep, wherein from meditation each participant gradually moves through a series of objectives bringing them to a sweat. After the Physical Warm-Up, emotional flexibility is challenged through an activity called POLARIZTIONS. Polarity, in this context, refers to specific internal contraries that are actually polar expressions of the same energy. Examples include: Safety/Danger, Victory/Defeat, Right/Wrong, Good/Evil, Pleasure/Pain, etc. These contraries are drawn from all possible arenas: Political, Conceptual, Social, Psychic, Etc., for accessing polarity and uniting opposition therein. **The intent is in initiating acquaintance with our Changing Whole.** Our Emotional Ego is liberated by finding out **where it's stuck ...** which side of a polarity it has identified with, at the cost of losing touch with the other side. The Flexible Ego is one capable of traversing between opposites **without becoming residential to either side...** while revealing the conversion points responsible for their overall unity (as the traditional myths of Hermes reflect).

A useful conceptual task is creating a list of charged polarities...those particular opposites which personally incite major resistance and/or excitement. Both negatively **and** positively charged polarities are essential for real work, due to the interlocking functions of both currents. Positive energy is more electrical and negative, magnetic. Together, they make up the electromagnetic field of our whole energy or, ***aura.*** . Too much positive excites a buoyancy that "ungrounds" us, unless it's balanced with an appropriate level of the stabilizing negative force. Too much negative collapses into a kind of "black hole" effect, wherein we feel trapped within ourselves and tending to suck others into our deep, dark predicament. Throughout ritual work, the process of balancing and merging opposites continues as a non-stop procedure...as the universe is always changing and calling for our continual adjustments.

During the process of POLARIZATIONS, one invariably encounters multitudes of ideas, pictures and other "socially-accepted" ideals of what that experience "should be or look like." For example, there are scores of images in our psyche constituting ideal Feminine and Masculine **models.** The conceptual challenge is in paying attention to how these obscure direct contact with the underlying forces, or Archetypes, of Feminine/Masculine. Encountering stereotypes is natural to breaking through the crust of our conditioned personality. Sometimes, all we can do is live through our ideations before **being touched and moved** by the wordless, intuitive opening of direct contact with their originating source. Other times, we are called to Drop Our Acts and **personify** these False Icons by suffering the embarrassment of purging them out. This journey's destination is through the very heart of our experience and out the other side. As we peel away the layers of cultural bias, we find our own responses and feelings **enabling the generation our own unique culture, tradition and cosmology.**

With practice, POLARIZATIONS proffer an internal cohesion expressing the totality of ourselves. A war within ourselves is gradually replaced by a consistent interplay of contraries, as we learn to permit the Spiritual. Once we learn the habit of accepting both sides of our nature, a self-support system develops... inviting greater challenge, expansion and growth. The ideal conditions for human growth and renewal seem to thrive around polarizations. Alchemically speaking, **our Body is the vessel** containing and mixing the opposites we experience. These oppositions are organically dissoved within us and enter the biological crucible of change, our LAB, (Read UNDOING YOURSELF by CS Hyatt; Falcon Press) wherein they coagulate, ferment, distill and transform themselves into a new substance altogether...one indigenous and inclusive of both sides of our nature. The fruit of this new quality is expanded consciousness and the working knowledge of relativity, or transcendence.

Through ritual, we become aware of our participation as alchemical crucibles for the delicate process of our personal refinement. Part of the reason for Sanctification is to protect and respect our internal transmutations. Consideration is also needed to guard our experiment from the extraneous and accidental impositions of Other People's Opinions, Useless Dispersion, and our own Personal Meddling & Rationalization of a process best suited for Nature Herself to govern. Especially fragile are those phases wherein nothing **seems** to be happening. Here, people tend to push and contrive themselves the most in order to **make something happen. It takes a genuinely reverent attitude to not resist the void.** As a general rule, when there's nothing happening on the surface, it's all cooking down below in the deeper recesses of our being. Our Self-commitment is put to work by staying with whatever is happening, despite our impatience for immediate, visible results.

CONVERSION POINTS

Perhaps the most mysterious (and fascinating) areas of ritual work involve those triggering mechanisms producing altered states of consciousness. From mild trance-dancing to the more cataclysmic mystical experiences, a spectrum of **conversions** is awakened in our souls. These **peak moments** seem to occur during an *amplification* of our current state of being. An acceleration of What Is often has the profound effect of synchronizing one state of being into a higher level of that being. There are innumerable forms of conversion experience, several of which appear to run common to this approach to ritual-making. One example engages our definitions of **control.** Control usually implies: Being In Charge, Directing Our Lives and/or Having a Firm Grip On Things. Indeed these are valid descriptions of an evolutionary phase control takes, especially in its initial stages of development.

When is the best time to shape reality and when is it appropriate to be shaped by it? If we're really in control, can we relax control when it's appropriate to do so? **We are shapers and we are the shaped.** Ritual often invites energetic intensification. In the midst of a greater energy than we are usually accustomed, there are a variety of ways to respond: 1) Control or direct it; 2) Fight and resist it; 3) Work to ignore it; and/or 4) Serve it. **The conversion point between *directing the energy to serving it* marks the initiation of a major revelation...**

When we are in charge of determining the direction of an energy, our source of authority/power rests in the personal will of our ego. This is when Ego is The Boss. If we were to relax the tendency to determine the outcome, we might increase our awareness of **the energy itself** and its innate, autonomous direction. By relaxing control, space is created for energetic expression, whereby we may rely on it to guide and inform us of its inherent direction. This is where Spirit is The Boss. These two Bosses set up an effective polarity for ritual work. Surrendering control is difficult, risky business as it exposes our vulnerability. Our vulnerable, open self knows how to be touched, moved and even broken. Without it, however, we are as good as dead and our rituals...mechanistic parodies of what could've been.

One way of giving up control is in realizing the futility of our personal efforts. When confronted with severe limitations and the growing awareness of our immobilization, our despair and helplessness sometimes telegraphs our need to surrender. Hitting Bottom initiates a conversion if we don't fight being down **when we're already there.** Hitting Bottom expresses an "ego-death"...the collapse of a self-image that is and/or was sacred to oneself. It was sacred because of our identification with this image. We were too busy **being it** to recognize its illusory status as just another image, or creation of thought. The conversion from ego-identification to Self-embodiment occcurs through **disillusionment,** which is often the price paid for *illumination,* until we become responsible for adjusting our thoughts to coincide more with the innate. Occasionally, we dawn upon the possibility that we don't have to be anything at all...*nobody special, in other words.*

One way of telling the difference between Ego-Personality and Essence-Self, is that the former is *image-defined* and the latter, ***quality-expressive.*** When an image of a quality is in direct conflict with the living expression of that quality, an essential friction is revealed whereby we are **living a lie.** For example: The socially-accepted ideation for Positive Energy is that it's "good" and that Negative Energy is "bad". If we are willing to sacrifice these conditioned preconceptions, we might descend into the nucleus of Positive Energy only to find it being a **threat** in doses larger than we're used to (as with people loving us more than we're willing to love ourselves). Negative Energy might reveal itself **instructive** and stabilizing in its capacity to refer us *back to ourselves.* If, in the light of new revelations, we fail to align new ideas with our fresh experience, internal conflict is generated and, unless we put it to work, it drains our power. To confess where we are living a lie is **effective** and brings results. Self-exposure and continual updating of definitions are two prerequisites for conscious human evolution...a primary ritual concern.

Conversion also occurs wherever we relax the desire to create a certain, predetermined effect and instead, open ourselves up to being affected. Ritual is *preparation for grace* or, turning vulnerable to the influence of The Self: its qualities, attributes and aspects. Without any guarantees whatsoever, we are asked to render ourselves receptive to be shaped like clay in the hands of Self... to be created and directed in the outcome of Its preference. The Self is the artist/sculptor and the ego/vehicle, its medium of expression. This is why it's necessary for us to know why we wish to practice ritual of this kind. The surrender required must be **completely ones own conscious choice to do so.** All effective ritual prepares for this type of conversion... otherwise, they become products of ego itself. Advanced ritual practice involves a deepening service to the Self. With the help of the*refining* process engaging the ego-personality, it becomes an instrument for Self-expression. The Self, however, depends upon High Ego Integrity for conveying Its intent. It is through the various prep phases of Sanctification, Warming Up and Polarizations that we become **malleable enough to absorb the shock of Self-penetration without being violated in the interim.**

The discipline of introducing ego to Self necessitates a certain *tempering of the will,* so as to minimize the shock of defeat as the experience of Self is always a defeat for the ego. Temperance can be practiced through those activities which polarize the will. (See Directional and Nondirectional movement in the Transitory Run of Ritual Preparation.) A polarized will is capable of shaping reality and being shaped by it. It is strong and flexible enough to adjust to both orientations **at will** as it has defined ***strength as balance.*.** This type of will bends to that direction serving the Greatest Good... or the process of Waking Up to the Self. One side-effect of a polarized will is personal transparency. ***Are you willing to see through yourself?***

SETTING UP POLARIZATIONS

Polarization makes it possible to ***accumulate*** **the type of presence indigenous to Wholeness with the birth of a"third point" of reference.** This "third point" is demonstrated by how polarizations are set up in ritual work. The setting is divided in half, with one side of a polarity projected into each half, i.e., GOOD on the right and EVIL on the left. The center, dividing line is dedicated to NO-FORM. From NO-FORM, one enters one side and explores the consequences of being shaped and influenced by the living forces of GOOD (whatever they may be). After sufficient development, one moves to the other side and surrrenders to the living forces of EVIL (As stated earlier, these forces refer to those within each of us as living realities, ie., **where we're at with Good & Evil.)** After EVIL, one returns to GOOD. One alternates between GOOD and EVIL until an awareness develops independent of them both. This "third point" is beyond GOOD and EVIL... **it is beyond polarity.** It is Consciousness Itself... a signal from our ever-present but hardly realized constancy... what the enigmatic Dance Master & Philosopher G. I. Gurdjieff called the "I".

The transcendent function of ritual avails itself whenever we are given glimpses of seeing beyond ourselves. Miracles like this can only occur when our self-knowledge is sufficient enough to afford the total giving, or surrender, of self. First, however, we must have a "self" before we can give of it. The generation of this kind of self-consciousness awakens as we become more acquainted with the multi-dimensional beings that we are. Drawing from a multitude of polarities, trinities and other aspects of Self, we may ceremoniously approach self-consciousness through ritual practice. By working intentionally with these aspects, we gradually start the arduous task of personal integration... the Life Work weaving together fragmented strands of ourselves towards a patchwork wholeness. The more pieces of our puzzle we gather, the more we begin to realize what a puzzle we really are. Even when all the pieces are placed, **it's still a puzzle... a mystery to be lived and not a problem to be figured out.**

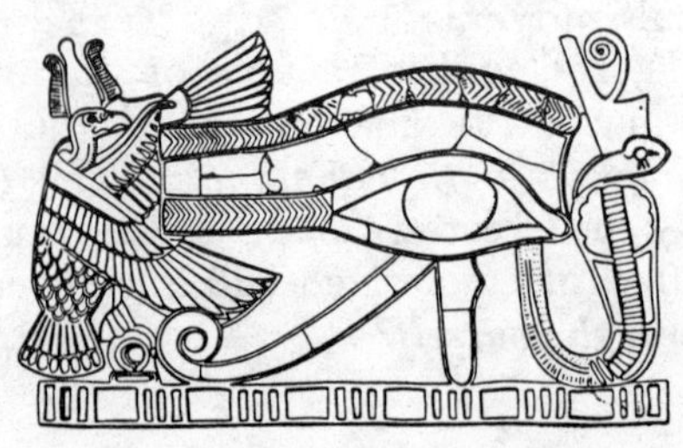

RITUAL PREPARATION

Guidelines For Entering Work

The following guidelines form the backbone to the dancing skeleton of ritual theatre. Its structure remains consistent for each ritual session. Personal freedom is found **within its form** by meeting the warm-up objectives **in ones own way**. ***The overall purpose of ritual preparation is in setting up a solid foundation for the evocation of spontaneous rituals.*** The basis of this foundation is the *accumulation of presence* through: **1) Feeling the body deeply 2) Emotional flexibility** and **3) Awareness.** Ritual garb is suggested to be **minimal and neutral**, i.e., sweat pants, tights and leotards, khaki/karate pants, t-shirts, and whenever possible...bare feet. Excessive jewelry gets in the way as does long hair that hasn't been tied or kept back. For obvious reasons, do not eat a large meal within two hours of the physical warm-up. Visit the restroom before setting up the RARE AREA unless you are fairly certain of maintaining sacred space while sitting on the toilet. Here now are listed the warm-up objectives to be met **on your own** towards designing a comprehensive ritual preparation:

I. **THE RARE AREA** -- an asocial orientation for entering ritual activities

II. **THE SETTING** -- physical location where ritual work takes place

III. **PRAYER CIRCLE** -- focal point for initiating group unity and devotion

IV. **SANCTIFICATION** -- collective service to the space of the setting

V. **THE POWER SPOT** -- process of finding your own space in the setting

VI. **THE LITTLE CIRCLE** -- cultivating self-dominion in your power spot

VII. **THE WARM-UP** -- a 40-60 minute period dedicated to designing ones own physical warm-up by meeting the objectives of **meditation, spinal flex, stretch**, and **sweat**...*according to personal style and freedom.*

VIII. **TRANSITORY RUN** -- jogging forms for marking transitions

IX. **POLARIZATIONS** -- ritual device for exciting emotional flexibility

X. **GROUP CIRCLE** -- convergence of participants for reflection

THE RARE AREA

A creative state initiates itself with SOLITUDE, the gratifying element of being alone...without which, true development is impossible. The ritual location is sanctioned as an Asocial Laboratory for testing our individual integrity or, Self-Commitment. In this spirit of experimentation, a RARE AREA functions to help us: 1) Leave the Social behind; 2) Permit internal dependence; and 3) Challenge the core of our being. A RARE AREA is **not** a place to party or come together for encounter or discourse about life. It is a time and space **set aside** for exploring the current shape and dynamic of our personality towards the eventual task of accessing its Source. Before Source Relations can unfold, it is crucial to be alone with oneself. Level One of ritual work is with establishing enough solitude to permit self-discovery. The acceptance of our fundamental aloneness and the realization we are working **for ourselves** , helps stabilize the RARE AREA.

THE SETTING

There are two potential settings, or ritual locations: INDOORS and OUTDOORS. To initiate this training process, INDOOR settings will be emphasized. (See GEOMANCY for Outdoor Ritual) Any indoor space will do so long as two major distractions are eliminated: **1) Things** (furniture, mirrors, wall hengings, etc.) and **2) Interruptions** (phones, visitors, etc.). A RARE AREA can be set up from anything as localized as your living room to a high school auditorium, just so you are **in charge of controlling the setting.** The setting requires enough SAFETY for participants to take the risks of becoming emotionally and psychically vulnerable. Room temperature should be unnoticable, so survival signals are not excited, i.e., too hot or too cold. The more neutral a space is, the easier it will be to own, sanctify and work in. The suggested lighting is on the dim side to minimize external stimulus (warm-up cycles have done very well in total darkness). Incense may be lit to facilitate sanctification and to make the space yours. (Frankincense, sage, cedar and copal are effective...see suggested reading under Temple Construction.)

THE PRAYER CIRCLE

After selecting the ritual setting, it is possible to initiate a prayer circle as a point of *focus* for Source Relations and Group Unity. Everyone should be in complete agreement to the prayer circle and if they are not, it should be bypassed until unanimous affinity is established. If the group is ready for a prayer circle, there are certain basic procedures to follow. A group circle is gathered in the center of the setting. Members prostrate themselves towards the circle's center. Since prayer is a highly personal, internal condition... instructions are received by simply getting down on your knees and praying. **The physical posture alone magnetizes the kind of receptivity conducive to initiating Source Relations and/or finding out where you're at with God.** Prayer circles are used to generate power for group sanctification of the ritual setting. The effectivenessof prayer depends entirely on **the quality and intensity of devotion** felt by each member for his/her source/god/diety within. The Heart Center (in the upper chest) and the Source Center (located above the head in space) can provide focal points between which devotional intensities may oscillate. Once devotion becomes almost "unbearable", one is ready to rise from the prayer circle and sanctify the space with the power penetrating oneself.

The prayer circle tends to work by itself and does not need external programs, affirmations, and/or goals beyond ones internal spiritual resonance. (The physical gesture of prostration is powerful enough on its own to evoke Source relations and/or resistance to same.) **A group unity develops from everybody's silent emotional commitment to God.** This is how we find *our own way* to the Source without having to convert others in the interim to ones private religious procedures. Thus, a spirit of "mutual autonomy" is encouraged and group members accepted more for **who they are** than for what they believe in or worship.

GROUP SANCTIFICATION

Group sanctification means collective service to the space of the ritual setting. After leaving the prayer circle, participants enter the surrounding space with the intent of *instilling safety throughout..* One way this occurs is by relating to the space itself as an entity, thus *charging it with value.* Sounds, gestures, movements honoring the element of **space itself** initiates the process of sanctification. This tends to instigate a sacred rapport due to the notion that **the space was there before anything else** and by honoring it, you place value on the source and origin of all things. The overall intent is in making this space **safe enough for everybody to be there.** The second phase of group sanctification is **owning it** while you are making it safe to be there. In this phase, individuals are owning the space **for the group** so collective rituals may occur there. There are a number of ways to do this and trial-and-error is the best. Guidelines include: 1) Making space holy enough to invite spiritual presence, thus making the space more sacred; 2) Including the presences and energetic directions of others during your individual activity of sanctification, i.e., accomodating them by creating more space **for their being** as you are physically approached by them; 3) Resonating sounds/melodies expressing prayer and extending these outward. Another useful device is designating the center of the ritual setting as an **optional** Prayer Circle, so that participants may enter this area throughout the initial process of Group Sanctification... coming and going as they wish.

THE POWER SPOT

After collective sanctification, individual members begin their process of finding POWER SPOTS, that area in the setting where (for reasons unknown) one feels good. There's an art to locating your Power Spot. It has to do with not looking for it but letting it **discover you and pull you to itself.** There are many ways to becoming receptive to its pull. One is shutting your eyes to slits so you begin moving through space SENSING for the area which FEELS BEST. Another is with shifting your point of attention down to your umbilical and/or solar plexus region and then, moving through the space while feeling for any tingling sensations in that zone. Still another method is letting your hands act as natural "radar scanners." Move through the space letting your hands do the sensing. If you look for Power Spots too directly, you might contrive the task. By **glancing askance,** your eyes find another way of seeing. Whatever you do here, **minimize rationalization and the analytical selection of the spot,** i.e., by a window or next to somebody you like. It's called a Power Spot for a reason and it starts the preparation for The Little Circle.

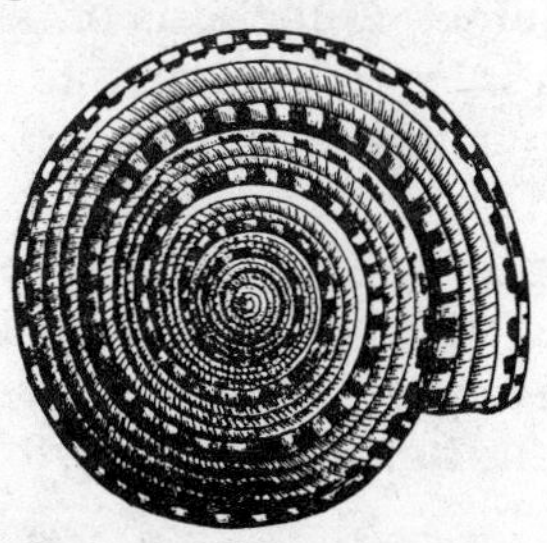

THE LITTLE CIRCLE

After individuals locate their Power Spots, the next ritual task is with the internal construction of The Little Circle. **The intent is in generating the ideal psychic atmosphere for ritual preparation while remaining in the confines of ones Power Spot.** This will help **contain** the process of gathering our forces. The Little Circle is articulated by **delineating the boundaries** of the Power spot: Physically, Emotionally and Psychically. After the boundaries are marked, the second task is with: 1) Sanctifying its space; and 2) Owning it completely. Like animals claim their territory, take total dominion over your spot. Explore those ways in which you naturally control space and take charge over it with movements, sounds and gestures expressing this process. The "energetic intent" here is **self-condensation**. The more of your presence you draw down into your Little Circle, the more tangible the ritual material. The overall objective of the Little Circle is in proferring the experience of being **SAFE AND ALONE. This way, everybody is responsible for generating their own safety, energy, and concentration.**

Two devices for stabilizing The Little Circle are: **1) Idiosyncratic Motion (IM); and 2) The Four Corners (TFC). IM** is any movement and/or gesture indigenous to our unique, singular self. These motions are idiosyncratic because only we would move in these ways. When they carry truth, no one will be able to duplicate them. They render us incomparable. **IM** conveys our "kinetic signature" and instills the Little Circle with the distinct energy of our personal freedom. **If it isn't fun, it's probably not working. Device #2, TFC** is more subtle and involves owning our space from a psychic level. It starts by standing in the center of the Circle and with eyes closed, visualizing/sensing the 360 degree peripherial boundary. Focus on a point directly in front of you at the periphery, then shift this point to the left side's periphery. Now, shift this point behind you to your "dorsal" boundary...then, shift it to your right boundary. Evaluate which point felt the faintest and **physically go there to vivify its existence somehow.** Go to the other points and physically establish each one. As you do this, be sensitive to potential **energetic functions** of these four corners. Each may have a specific quality or inherent energy unto itself. Does it elicit a certain response from yourself while you're there ? (See WILDERNESS by Julian Simeon in this book)

For example, one corner may evoke a defensive posture whileanother corner excites an open gesture and still another, a form of worship. Best not to have preconceptions save for the possibility of **TFC** possessing innate energetic functions serving to bond the Little Circle. (The technique of TFC has been used traditionally for aeons to create placement via The Four Directions of East, West, North and South... each with their various totems, allies and guiding spirits. For those wishing to evoke their own tradition, it is suggested practice to bypass preconceptions in general and instead, create a space to receive new information about the intrinsic meanings of The Four Directions.)

When our individual placement and presence is stabilized in the Little Circle, it's time to enter the PHYSICAL WARM-UP. There are four phases to the WARM-UP, each lasting between 10-15 minutes depending on personal and group decision before meeting. (A clock should be kept within eyes' distance or somebody appointed to mark time intervals with a sound or word.) The four phases are called: **MEDITATION, SPINAL FLEX, STRETCH** and **SWEAT**. Ideally, they unfold from one to the next as one continual motion towards ***feeling the body deeply...the overall objective of the Physical Warm-Up.***

MEDITATION

The intent here is maintaining any posture affording utter physical stillness for 10-15 minutes. The quality of stillness determines the quality of activity thereafter. Within the stillness, it is possible to sanctify the meditation either by entering NO-FORM and/or through silent prayer. Other keys include asking oneself, **"Why am I here?"** and **"What am I warming up and preparing for?"** Another internal task is in relaxing our desire to control and/or determine an outcome. The purpose of meditation is accumulating presence. In meditation, we may integrate conceptual intelligence by simply asking ourselves to **PAY ATTENTION TO ONLY THAT WHICH IS HAPPENING AND TO WHAT WE ARE DOING.**

SPINAL FLEX

From Meditation, move into a position to start start the gradual awakening of the Central Nervous System through the gentle flexing of the spinal cord. Don't neglect the areas located in the small of the back where vertebrae tighten together and the base of the skull. Basic Foot Reflexology demonstrates how the arches in each foot are connected to the spinal cord, whereby the area closer to the heel relates to the base of the spine and the area closer to the ball of the foot, the neck. Directly massaging these areas helps loosen the spine.

Another method of SPINAL FLEX is laying on your back with knees bent and arms out perpendicular to the torso. By resting against the floor, lift the bottom vertebrae up and keep lifting the spine ever so gradually... vertebrae by vertebrae...all the way to your neck. Then, just as gradually, unfold each vertebrae (one-by-one) back to the floor. Repetition of this spinal unfolding is a gentle way to loosen the spine. **Breathe continuously.** The breath vitalizes the body as it circulates its energy from within. Explore your own methods of SPINAL FLEX.

STRETCH

The intent with stretching is waking the body up. Scan the body for regions wherein you either feel nothing or feel numb. **Breathe and stretch** into these dead zones. We are stretching to reclaim our bodies and penetrate them with our intent through breathing and feeling. After initiating several minutes of stretching, begin owning your space with the way you're stretching. Recreate your boundaries if you've lost them. Connect stretching with breathing and take more dominion over the space. Stretch the unfelt regions of yourself. **Pay attention only to what you are doing.** If you automatically start "spacing out", do something immediately to *feel your body...like, become aware of the sensation in your right hand.* We are working through our resistances to being here and the degree of self-commitment required for this monumental task is just short of miraculous at times.

SWEAT

From Stretching, we move into those activities generating enough heat to break a sweat. This is best paced to minimize premature exhaustion. Movements producing heat are executed within the confines of the Little Circle while making efforts to **contain** ones heat rather than disperse it outwards. (Heat occurs when matter turns into spirit and spirit materializes. This phase is most essential as it re-awakens the intersection between spirit and body with the Holy Water of Sweat itself. **This is a time to accelerate our physical energy.)**

RHYTHM is a ritual function for stabilizing a continuity and presence into our movement. Through rhythm, it becomes easier to build a sweat and generate heat without premature exhaustion.

ALTERING THE EXPECTED is another ritual function, or device, to help the process of waking up the body. It starts with establishing a specific level of energy, movement, rhythm and sound... then, blending it or tossing oneself into an opposite level of energy, movement, rhythm and sound. This is a good way to start introducing **polarizations**... moving between opposites for the purpose of greater flexibility

OWN THE SPACE by the way you're generating heat. During the WARM-UP, ones boundaries tend to shift, expand and/or contract due to various energetic adjustments. SWEAT starts the end of the first major Warm-up Cycle and it is suggested to re-check your boundaries during this time. (If you need to adjust your boundaries to accomodate your expanding/contracting presence, this is an appropriate time.)

After SWEAT, return to the center of the Little Circle and gather your forces. Shrink/condense the boundaries of the Little Circle to your skin, so that **your body alone becomes the Little Circle, your sacred space.** You are now prepared for the TRANSITORY RUN. The following section presents numerous jogging forms. Select one or two to practice after the WARM-UP period of each ritual session. TRANSITORY RUNS are "set-ups" for POLARIZATIONS.

THE TRANSITORY RUN

THE TRANSITORY RUN is a vehicle for marking change and checking equillibrium. After the 4-phase warm-up, participants jog around the periphery of the ritual setting...sustaining everthing generated while warming up. **The primary intent of THE TRANSITORY RUN is furthering our flexibility, concentration and skill through jogging forms.** There are numerous shapes THE TRANSITORY RUN takes, some of which are presented hereafter. New shapes will invariably emerge once the overall objective is understood through actual practice. Here are a series of TRANSITORY RUNS:

1) Shift awareness to left hand. Right foot. Left elbow. Right knee. Entire left side of body. Right side. Let the jog be influenced by points of focus. This challenges **one-pointedness of attention** and the ability to shift or mobilize ones consciousness to different areas.

2) Gather attention to a point at the energy center, or chakra, dominating your current state of being. Let the jog be affected by this center, so its energetic influence **permeates your whole body.** Shift to other centers and repeat procedures. Energy evaluation task.

3) Project attention point 3 feet above head; let it influence jog. Shift point to 3 feet in front of you; jog influenced. Shift point 3 feet below you; jog influenced. Shift point 3 feet behind you; jog influenced. Shift to left, then shift it to the right. Now, project SIX CARDINAL POINTS: above, below, front, back, left and right. Let them simultaneously effect the jog. Draw a line from each point converging them all into a central body location that is not predetermined. Jog from this central point. Let point expand, filling the body, so eventually the whole body BECOMES THE POINT. Move through space ***as the point.*** Align with Body Consciousness and move **as a unit.**

4) Project sphere of SOURCE ENERGY above head. Draw down a column of this energy into your crown and down through your spine and into the earth. Jog in the center of this column. **Source Relations device.**

5) Visualize a horizontal plane 5 feet above head that stretches out to infinity in all directions. Gradually, command the plane to descend to the level of the top of your head, so this body area is awakened. Then, gradually, let it descend down to the levels of your BROW, THROAT, STERNUM, SOLAR PLEXUS, NAVEL, PELVIS, THIGHS, KNEES, ANKLES, FEET, and finally coincide the plane to THE FLOOR ITSELF.

6) Project a sphere of SOURCE ENERGY above you head, as in **#4.** Let the energy therein be VIOLET before drawing it down into the column run-down through you body and into the earth. From VIOLET, let it turn BLUE...then GREEN...then YELLOW...then ORANGE...then RED...let the red darken to crimson, burgundy, indigo and on into BLACK. Let each color influence the jog even if it **immobilizes** the jogging itself into the BLACK.

7) Locate area of body that feels vague or numb. Let this area become heavy by **shifting your center of gravity** there. When this area is distinguished, shift the gravity to another vague area. Repeat.

8) Discover your present-time relationship with **The Earth** and express this via jogging. Determine how much you wish to participate and commit to this relationship and **let your commitment determine the direction** and quality of the jogging. Feel free to resonate sounds.

9) Express present-time RESISTANCE via jogging, sounds, etc. until you **get it out of your system** enough to move on to more commitment.

10) Expand your aura to fill the room; jog from its center. Contract your aura to a few inches outside of your skin. **Oscillate** between auric expansion and contraction until you discover your point of balance.

11) Visualize being inside a hollow chamber with no bottom or top. Let it **amplify and contain** your solitude.

12) Without changing anything, let any IMBALANCE come forth to shape the jog and dominate it to the point of rendering you immobilized. Let the immobilization become a "statue" expressing the outcome of that particular imbalance. After extracting the "message" of this frozen form, shake it loose and continue jogging to repeat this process three times...each time redefining your POINT OF BALANCE in light of previous imbalances. **Discover strength as balance.**

13) Jog in a semi-NO-FORM state, eyes open a slit. Project your own consciousness out of your body above your head, creating the effect of an Empty Shell of a Body jogging below you. Watch youself jog from above your body. Then, enter your crown, owning it. Descend into each chakra, **owning each as you go.** Recall those chakras you were unable to claim as yours. Consider this information as a basis for future ritual material.

14) Pay attention to any energetic and/or social contracts impeding the capacity to be in present time. Jog in a way to **release** these obligations, energies and agreements so you can deal with them later. Radiate any energy not innate to yourself... radiate it out and away.

15) Don't pay attention to anything in particular. **Just run for the hell of it.**

16) Designate each side, or wall, of the workspace as charged with the spirit of one of THE FOUR ELEMENTS, so that each time you run along side you are influenced by that spirit. Pay attention to the **transitions** between each element and the **conversion points therein.**

17) Feel the bottoms of your feet from the inside, so your attention shifts from FOOT to FLOOR contact and into "internal foot" to sole contact. Practice GRIPPING and LETTING GO. (This connects soul-consciousness to sole reality.)

The last and perhaps most effective form of TRANSITORY RUN, is the practice of **DIRECTIONAL** and ***NON-DIRECTIONAL*** **MOVEMENT.** They are defined as such:

<u>DIRECTIONAL</u> -- movement that is completely **determined** by the personal will of the one moving; elements of the jog under the movers control are coordinates of TENSION, STYLE, SPEED and *self-determined motion in its absolute sense.*

<u>NON-DIRECTIONAL</u> -- movement initiated by the **impulses** of the organism; set into motion by releasing the grip on ones body to "let the animal run"; the degree of abandonment possible without harming oneself and/or others.

Both forms of movement can be reinforced through sonic resonance...those sounds expressing the internal state of the orientation in command. To test your capacity for both, start out in DIRECTIONAL movement and see how much control you have over your body by determining its TENSION, STYLE, SPEED AND RHYTHM. Then, at your point of peak control, let go of the grip you have on your body. **Abandon control and let the body run.** (This is a subtle process as there is no way of really controlling abandonment at this early phase...only genuine surrender of control works.) At your point of peak abandonment, **follow a random motion into DIRECTIONAL movement and design a new jogging form** with a totally different set of coordinates (new TENSION, STYLE, SPEED and RHYTHM). *Take more control than before.* Let this new form crystallize until it just about immobilizes you, then release your grip and fall **deeper into abandonment** than before. At your peak abandonment, follow a random motion into DIRECTIONAL again with a new set of coordinates taking even MORE CONTROL. Repeat this oscillation 3-5 times, or when you've had enough, and then initiate a jog combining both orientations towards a kind of **CONTROLLED ABANDONMENT.** Then, slow this down to a walk. Pare away any excess gesturing/posturing to refine a Normal Pedestrian Walk (discreet) yet, still expressive of your point of balance.

The Transitory Run functions to mark transitions. It can be applied between actual rituals themselves for the purpose of restoring balance and/or just putting oneself through changes. Overall, the Transitory Run is a device for *recognizing/integrating change.*

POLARIZATIONS

Up to this point in the ritual prep, internal emphasis has been somewhat minimal, with the exceptions of Sanctification and owning the Little Circle. Predominately, it has been a physical warm-up to feel the body deeply. In this next phase, **the intent is with emotional flexibility.** The primary focus is total reliance on an inner source of stimulus and information. There is a secondary emphasis on outward expression of what one is impressed by internally. Before proceeding to POLARIZATIONS, three additional ritual functions need introducing. They are: 1) **NO-FORM**; 2) **PROJECTION**; and 3) **CONTACT POINT**.

Without the integration of these crucial functions, the following ritual designs, floor plans and reference points become ludicrous and the rituals, lifeless. In POLARIZATIONS, they are activated and "primed" so we may enter ritual work *already catalyzed.*

The mechanics involved in setting up POLARIZATIONS are as such: After returning from the Transitory Run, relocate in the Little Circle to re-claim and sanctify its space. Once done, step outside its boundaries while facing the circle. Here, enter NO-FORM. From NO-FORM, we PROJECT a charged polarity into the circle and then enter that circle to surrender to its influence. **The CONTACT POINT is that area in your body and/or your aura where you feel the most direct, open-ended influx of the force previously PROJECTED into the Little Circle.** The intent is locating this CONTACT POINT and dedicating your whole self to absorbing the force through it. This is the Self-commitment refered to earlier and it determines the quality and depth of your work.

DRAWING DOWN POLARITY

From NO-FORM, project one side of the polarity you wish to work with into the Little Circle. Enter the circle and give yourself totally to its influence. Remain until it becomes an encompassing sensation wherein that quality permeates every part of you. Upon immersion, serve the direction of the quality by its expression through you as Sound, Gesture, Motion, Etc. When you feel complete with it, step back outside the Little Circle and return to the NO-FORM stance. When you have neutralized the quality through immersion in No-Form, project its opposite into the circle (some of the more charged qualities may be difficult to release...breathe and let the Earth absorb and process it for you. (see Dangers of Ritual)

After projecting the opposite quality into the circle, enter in and surrender to its influence until it becomes an encompassing feeling. When complete, step outside the circle and return to NO-FORM. From NO-FORM, see the circle before you. Visualize or sense a line down the middle of it, creating two halves in your whole circle. Project your whole polarity into the circle, one side to each half. Do not decide which half to enter first. Instead, stand between both halves and let the side exerting the strongest "pull" invite you in. (If your No-Form is true enough, you will be receptive to the pull.) Once in, explore each side thoroughly until the NEED for the other compels your entry into that side. Let your NEED FOR THE OTHER determine the timing of your entries into each half. Move between sides, alternating your "current" and raising your awareness to new levels of each side of the whole. When complete, return to NO-FORM. (After some practice, it is possible to forgo the first part and simply project both sides of the polarity into the Little Circle at once).

GROUP POLARIZATIONS

The entire ritual setting is divided in half with the mid-section designated as THE CORRIDOR OF NO-FORM. Here participants line up single file with the polarity projected to their left and right sides. They enter the side exerting the pull. Feel free to relate to others as a way of enforcing the side you're in. Experiment with alternating your current and passing through the CORRIDOR OF NO-FORM. Oscillate, as a group, between both sides of the setting. Return to NO-FORM when you feel complete.

NO-FORM

The NO-FORM stance starts with any standing position supporting yourself and affording balance. Knees are **unlocked**. The head **rests** on the neck, which rests on shoulders resting on torso...and so forth, all the way down to your feet resting on the floor. This is a stance supporting **total rest.** Internally, two things are happening: 1) You withdraw your attention, energy and identification from the environment and connect these within yourself; and...2) Emphasize the **exhale,** so the inhale occurs on its own without your help or awareness. Close the eyes half way or to slits to **minimize external stimulus.** Your body may need to go through various "ticks and jerks" as its way of adjusting. You may want to shake yourself, take deep breaths and do anything internally to **permit nothingness.** There are ingrained, conditioned resistances to NO-FORM that may emerge for your scrutiny. If you are able and willing, look at them and then, let them go. With each release, breathe deep and exhale. This is the time to **Drop Your Act** and fall into the depths of your groundless being.

THE CLOUD OF UNKNOWING

The CLOUD OF UNKNOWING meditation serves as a bridge to NO-FORM if you are unable and/or unwilling to be nothing. Enter the No-Form stance as described previously and initiate your own process of "hollowing out" or becoming nothing. Then, visualize/sense/project a cloud of "pure NO-FORM energy" 3-5 feet above your head. Let this cloud be slightly larger than your body. Permit this CLOUD OF UNKNOWING to hover suspended above your head, while you maintain your hollow state below. When you feel you've exhausted your resources for hollowing out, invite the CLOUD OF UNKNOWING down and let it enter your crown, so just your head is inside the cloud. After a few moments, gradually draw the cloud down to encompass your entire body...all the way to the floor. Feel the cloud totally encompassing your body so, *you are in a cloud of pure NO-FORM energy.* Now, let this cloud penetrate your skin everywhere and begin permeating your entire body. Feel the NO-FORM everywhere. **Become the void.** Discover how comfortable you can be by resting in the void...resting in your true nature. The moment your No-Form is **most true,** you are ready for **charging** the ritual through **conscious projection.**

CONSCIOUS PROJECTION

Two common impediments to intentional Projection are: 1) ***Preconceptions/premeditations;*** **and 2)** ***Judgment.*** We are looking to Project the pure signal of, let's say, the color "RED". If we insist on a certain shade of red or judge the color as not our "favorite" this *static* will be fused with the projection. Then, you will explore your preconceptions and judgments along with the pure signal of RED. There's nothing wrong with this per se. This is a demonstration of how we determine our projections. We will tend to experience whatever we send in. Without preconceptions,the element of surprise is activated. Even with judgmental projections, the Unexpected will emerge...it's just that you may have to work through your stuff first.

Whatever is projected refers to its current reality within ourselves. For example,if you project LOVE/FEAR into the circle...you will experience how your body registers its current contact with these forces...or, where you're now at with love and fear. If you have a lot of ideations about these, they will also tend to surface. If your concepts do not coincide with your body's living relationship with these forces, you manifest conflict and the drama of your "ritual material". Ritual work involves moving through our ideas and into their underlying governing forces, so that we might realign our images to synchronize with the the innate. This is what has been refered to as the complete transformation of the mind. The process is not easy and requires total self-commitment...dedication to finding out **for oneself** the nature of the forces governing our existence, so we might live a deeper, higher life. It is the conflict between Ego and Self, Personality and Essence, Idea and Quality... which provides the "food" for the formation of a New Self and the awareness of our needs to transform.

CONTACT POINT

The Contact Point can be used with or without projecting a quality into a circle, as previously presented. One locates the contact point with, let's say, "that which is most true" while you are standing in NO-FORM. The Contact Point is that area in your body and/or aura providing direct, intuitive absorbtion with "that which is most true" to yourself. One internal adjustment for amplifying the Contact Point comes with **creating space within you for the expression of the quality evoked.** Upon its expression within this space, find the most effective way to follow and/or serve **its** direction. **The intent of the Contact Point is with sensitizing us to the innate energetic direction of a given quality.** We are asked to **permit** the **autonomy** of the quality evoked so it can *have a life of its own.*

(In context with Projection, the Contact Point is the area you feel the quality entering you as you enter the area where your projection was directed. Through total commitment to the Contact Point, we are growing "true to our source" and start to recognize the feeling of this kind of internal loyalty. With practice, this feeling grows and Source becomes more accessible. Source Relations begin by with our steady commitment to the Contact Point.)

POLARITIES

The following sets of polarities can be used for polarizations and/or the basis of ***complete rituals unto themselves..*** Underline the polarities which excite a big resistance **and** circle the ones creating definite excitement. These are your **charged** polarities and will do much to introduce you to your internal material, from which actual rituals can be constructed. If you haven't already done so, you might want to list additional polarities more personal to yourself. **The more** ***personal*** **they are, the closer you get to initiation.**

POSITIVE -- NEGATIVE
MASCULINE -- FEMININE
CONTRACTION -- EXPANSION
INNOCENCE -- EXPERIENCE
RESISTANT -- YIELDING
RADIANT -- MAGNETIC
DRY -- MOIST
STRONG -- WEAK
ORDER -- CHAOS
HOT -- COLD
ANGULAR -- CURVACIOUS
FIXED -- MUTABLE
BOTTOM -- TOP
RED -- GREEN
ORANGE -- BLUE
YELLOW -- VIOLET
GOLD -- SILVER
IMPORTANT -- INSIGNIFICANT
NOURISHMENT -- POISON
STABLE -- VOLATILE
DOMINANT -- SUBMISSIVE
MARS -- VENUS
SUN -- MOON
CENTER -- PERIPHERY
VIRTUE -- SIN
GRAVITY -- ELECTRICITY
SATIATED -- HUNGRY
KNOWN -- UNKNOWN
MECHANICAL -- SPONTANEOUS
GRACE -- INTENTION
PETTY -- SIGNIFICANT

GOOD -- EVIL
SOCIAL -- THEATRICAL
PLEASURE -- PAIN
YOUNG -- OLD
TIME -- SPACE
HEAVEN -- HELL
COMMITMENT -- INDIFFERENCE
REWARD -- PUNISHMENT
SAFETY -- DANGEROUS
HUMOR -- DEFENSIVENESS
IGNORANCE -- WISDOM
VICTORY -- DEFEAT
SULPHER -- PHOSPHOROUS
LACK -- ABUNDANCE
BEAUTY -- UGLINESS
MERCY -- SEVERITY
REASON -- INTUITION
HEAD -- GUT
RIGHT -- WRONG
PRECISE -- SLOPPY
CONCENTRATED -- DISPERSED
INTOXICATED -- SOBER
HEART -- HEARTLESS
HEALTH -- ILLNESS
LOVE -- FEAR
ISOLATION -- COMMUNION
GUILT -- PRIDE
PARENT -- CHILD
DEEP -- SHALLOW
HARD -- SOFT
MUNDANE -- COSMIC

EFFECTIVE -- INEFFECTIVE
CREATURE -- SPIRIT
JOY -- SORROW
AGONY -- ECSTACY
CREATIVE -- DESTRUCTIVE
EMBODIED -- DISINCARNATE
ATTACHMENT -- DETACHMENT
DENSITY -- CLARITY
ILLUSION -- REALITY
SEEING -- FEELING
VALUE -- WORTHLESS
SURPRISE -- PLANNED
FAILURE -- SUCCESS
PERFECTION -- FLAW
STUPID -- CLEVER
PRIMITIVE -- SOPHISTICATED
SILENCE -- NOISE
SERVICE -- IDENTITY
SENSITIVITY -- NUMBNESS
SANITY -- INSANITY
RELATIVE -- ABSOLUTE
DEFENSIVE -- VULNERABLE
OPEN -- CLOSED
PRESSURE -- SPACIOUSNESS
PRESENCE -- ABSENCE

SACRED -- PROFANE
PERSONAL -- IMPERSONAL
ROOTED -- GROUNDLESS
FREEDOM -- SLAVERY
FOOL -- MAGUS
RISING -- FALLING
EXTERNAL -- INTERNAL
EXCITEMENT -- RESISTANCE
OBLIVIOUS -- OBSERVANT
DIFFICULT -- EASY
DIRECT -- INDIRECT
DESIRE -- APATHY
ENCHANTMENT -- DISILLUSIONMENT
ACCEPTANCE -- DENIAL
DEAD -- ALIVE
DECEPTION -- HONESTY
CRUELTY -- SYMPATHY
CONTROL -- ABANDONMENT
SIMPLE -- COMPLEX
CHANCE -- PURPOSE
UNCERTAINTY -- CERTAINTY
CALM -- UPSET
REPULSION -- ATTRACTION
ARRIVAL -- DEPARTURE
DOING -- BEING

THE GROUP CIRCLE

The purpose of The Group Circle is in providing a brief period for assimilating what has transpired so the group may proceed en masse to the next ritual. After polarizations of the solo and/or group kind, it's often useful to convene in the center of the setting. This has several functions, the primary being a focused transition point *between* rituals. After the emotional warm-up of polarizations, participants meet in the circle to voice comments necessary for them to **proceed with the work.** It has proven effective to keep these comments brief, direct and to the point. **Another value seems to be encouraging a spirit of non-judgment towards self and/or others.** It is simply a time to communicate What Happened for the purpose of checking in and digesting...stomaching the experience.

If there is a Ritual Catalyst, this is a good time to scan the overall energy levels of the group mind and of each individual for determining the appropriate ceremony to enter. What we're looking for is whatever **amplifies present-time dynamics** and triggers the next phase of evolution and development. This is a crucial point to understand. Otherwise, the catalyst runs the risk of imposing his/her own ideals onto the actual group gestalt. It takes a perceptive person to distinguish between the present ongoing reality and our projections and expectations on same. (See Ritual Catalyst section). It's also a good idea to come together in THE GROUP CIRCLE after a particularly charged or long set of rituals. Due to the kind of depth experience ritual often invokes, the element of TALKING is important to help dissipate the charge often accumulated. Talking can integrate "right-brain" **experience** with "left-brain" **description** for the purpose of psychological assimilation. Talking and laughing also break up fixations sometimes occuring after intense ritual. The primary concern of Group Circles is remembering to stay close to **what actually happened,** rather than spin off into philosophical discourse, personal problems or socializing. This will minimize tendencies for inflaming encounter therapy sessions (unless that is what you want). *There's a fine line between psychological integration and pissing your power away.*

If the group is advanced in ritual work or familiar enough with themselves, the Group Circle is a good time to determine which rituals to proceed with based on what has transpired. Rituals can be constructed by combining issues often emerging throughout the Warm-Up and/or selected from the following RITUAL DESIGN section.

RITUAL FUNCTIONS

An Association of Techniques

The following techniques provide adjustments for enhancing ritual integrity. It is suggested practice to select and experiment with one everytime one enters ritual work in order to understand their combined value. Like any disciplinary technology, the methods need to be absorbed before their integration occurs as instinctual response, or "second nature."

ATTENTION

Interruptions tend to undermine concentration and disperse valuable accumulated presence. Continuity of consciousness is essential for ritual integrity. The intensity and duration of your attention determines the **quality** of your work. Distractions can be integrated in various ways. Arbitrary sounds and audio disturbance will enhance your work if you make the necessary internal adjustments to refer to these as **The Soundtrack...an audio backdrop for the material.** Dispersions of the Spacing Out variety can be eliminated by training yourself to: **1) Register when this is happening; and 2) Focus into the senation of your hand or foot.** From here, any further concentration towards FEELING YOUR BODY draws the presence back again. **Sensation** is an entry point to SPACING IN, when you catch yourself doing the opposite. PAY ATTENTION TO ONLY WHAT YOU ARE DOING. Sustaining a continuity of consciousness will eventually connect The Eternal and initiate magick.

CONTAINMENT

Containment is a ***anti-dispersion device.*** It requires a strong sense of personal boundaries, i.e., the borders of the Little Circle and/or your Aura itself. Boundaries do not refer to visualized or imagined walls, defense mechanisms or arbitrary borders. **Boundaries are the outer edge of your emanation.** Discover how much space you fill and where your energy joins the void at its periphery. Containment implies sustaining your attention and presence **within your own aura or energetic field.** A way of testing containment is through radiating your energy out to its outer limits and letting it BOUNCE BACK to affect you at the center (of the aura). Being affected by ones own emanation helps develop familiarity with ones own energy. **Subject yourself to being under the influence of your own emanations.**

RESONANCE

Resonance connects Source with the Personality. It is the capacity for registering your current frequency, or energy level, and matching a sound to give vocal expression to that level. It is **not** creating a sound or determining its outcome. Instead, resonance commits itself to serving the expression of the source, or contact point, involved. This activates the energy center in the base of the throat and sets up communication lines between Person and Essence. The throat is a "sacred chamber" interconnecting The Head with The Rest of The Body. Resonating opens the chamber doors so Spirit may pass down to join Body and that Body may aspire to meet Spirit. **Matching the energy with a sound...** (Also see VOCAL CREATIONS section)

SANCTIFICATION OF RESISTANCE

Resistance is frozen energy. It's usually found in a specific location in the body and/or an overall sense of tension. It's frozen energy because some aspect of Self has been judged as being WRONG and NOT O.K. the way it is, and so an accumulative inhibition develops around it. Often times, resistance itself is *resisted,* thus generating more tension and body/psychic armor. **Sanctifying resistance means not judging it when it comes up, and instead relating to it as a source of energy: *a contact point.*** Surrender to this source and let your body/voice serve its expressions, no matter how twisted, contorted and gnarly they get. Resonating with resistance helps break it up for accessing as well. Resistance is not different than Life and awaits inclusion along with the rest of yourself.

DEVELOPMENT

During actual work, DEVELOPMENT is essential for *ending and beginning cycles.* The element of **follow-through** permits us to stay with whatever is happening for the purpose of **development** and its articulation of evolutionary phases of metamorphosis. Follow-through is especially helpful during those moments where Nothing is Happening, whereby we Stick With It until something new emerges. Development is a test to self-commitment and overall integrity. It encourages us to stay with what's happening No Matter What...even if it dies and changes on us, **we're right there with it.** Each contact point contains its cycles and these can be revealed only through our dedication to development. Through development, we permit expression to extend and unfold to its natural conclusions and... potential re-emergence.

GESTURE

Gesture is a ritual function for expressing and containing the power of peak moments. During ritual development there emerges certain moments of truth which we'll call "peaks." In these moments, an obvious amplification occurs...increasing intensity of energy and clarity of form. **Gesture crystallizes the essence of a quality through the whole body as a form, posture and/or statue.** Gesture frames peak moments as a way of synchronizing mind (attention) and body into a singular, cohesive direction. When the body gives itself totally to gesture, it turns into a living symbol encoding the contained essence into its cellular memory for future recall. A series of such gestures forms the development of personal/collective mythology as a living code for transmitting intensity. **Myth is the language of essences constructed from an evolution, or development, of gestures.**

CONVERSION

Conversion is the transformation point wherein one distinct quality or state turns into another. This often occurs after complete commitment to a particular condition resulting in the conversion to its opposite. Another conductor for conversion can be found in those rituals where the outcome remains completely unpredictable. Our capacity for **permitting uncertainty** is preliminary to transformation from one "reality tunnel" into another. **Conversion points** can be discovered amidst any ritual where **development** and follow-through are established as **constant values.**

SACRIFICE

The ritual function of sacrifice releases great psychic energy. Sacrifice means "to make sacred" by an offering. Effective sacrifice releases "what is most dear to our hearts" and where we are **identified.** Sacrificial icons are often found in those areas where **we love something or someone we have outgrown.** Sacrifice implies letting go of attachment. Before sacrifice is understood and expressed, the attachment must be located. Initiation rituals exploring ones Point of Worship, The Deity Within, Etc., can activate this awareness of bondage. A key to understanding sacrifice is that what is usually held sacred is an image or thought **about** GOD, SELF and/or REALITY and **not** *the living presence itself.* These icons are images falsely identified as the Deity Within and so they are subject to sacrifice. Another attribute which is subject to offering is **the will itself** and our *unwillingness* to relax our desire to control and predetermine outcomes.

PRAYER

Prayer is a gesture crystallizing the essence of our rapport with the Deity Within. Certain forms and postures are more conducive to catalyzing living communion and dialogue with Source than others. Due to the highly personal nature of these forms, none are suggested, yet experimentation is highly encouraged. To locate them, enter those rituals set up for dialogue with Source and apply the ritual function of GESTURE.

RHYTHM

Rhythm is a ritual function for expressing patterns of energy through movement and sonic resonance. It is a self-reference device helping to restore our placement when ritual amplification intensifies. The pulse and breath of rhythm is also a doorway through trance and losing ourselves. Rhythm is also a device for magnetizing group synchronization. Either way, rhythm articulates the current patterns of motion passing through ourselves during ritual.

INTERPLAY

Group interplay is a ritual function when individuals remain commited to their current contact point before, during and after interaction with others. It is with the *interplay of forces* that ritual develops **on its own.** This occurs as long as each participant remains true to their "vertical" Source (by dedication to their contact points) while relating to the "horizontal" plane of human interactions. If you are thrown off and lose touch with your Source at anytime, stop everything and ***return to NO-FORM and begin again.***

ECONOMY

Economy implies any adjustment made to eliminate arbitrary movement...expression unessential to conveying a particular quality. This can be implemented by focusing on **micro-movements**...locating your point of minimal expression during a ritual. It means emphasizing the Small, and bypassing tendencies towards dramatic display of feeling, sound and gesture. Economy is especially useful for the purpose of **containment** of energies and their re-direction *through the flesh itself,* instead of outward radiation. It takes more awareness to exercise economy than not...

DESIGN

Design is a kinetic device for clarifying the physical forms evolving from commitment to an internal contact/source. The advanced work of design entails disidentifying oneself enough from the forces at play to recognize their evolving forms, shapes and patterns. Design is the internal/external adjustment of clarifying and "cleaning up" physical directions that emerge without killing their energetic integrity. In this way, higher dance forms develop from initial patterns experienced from the contact point engaged. When these patterns are clarified, the design element is expressed and a choreography, begun.

CHARACTERIZATION

Advanced ritual theatre work. There are predominantly three stages of work: **1) Experience; 2) Design; and 3) Characterization and Story.** The first phase requires emotional surrender and the complete giving of oneself without paying attention to effect or outcome. This is the stage of raw, indulgent (sloppy) experience so essential for Self-Initiation. The second stage explores kinetic designs emerging from the experience of the first phase for their clarification and eventual choreography. The third stage engages character development, story and mythology integrating the previous two stages, so its energetic and structural integrity remain intact.

Characterization involves the extension of an internal source into the body to form a WALK, a MASK, and a PURPOSE. For the sake of authenticity, these must evolve from **the contact point** and **not** created or affected by personal efforts. Through the process of INTERPLAY, the character develops an understanding of his/her myth, or story. This often occurs with Source Relations first and then, is tested with other characters. The myth clarifies as the character surrenders to his/her destiny by realizing its PURPOSE. **Purpose manifests through knowing what you want and how to get it and there are two levels of PURPOSE: 1) Near; and 2) Far.** Near purpose is what the character wants ***moment-to-moment*** and Far purpose, what character hopes to accomplish ***in the long run***...the Big Picture. As with all INTERPLAY, participants are challenged to sustain internal dependence *via the contact point.* If at any time we become overly influenced by another person's force and/or field, it is suggested practice to stop and return to NO-FORM for restoring your contact with Source.

SERVICE

The ritual function of service can be used amidst great uncertainty for establishing placement in a new territory. Once ushered into a new region, whether it be physical-emotional-psychic,there is often a confusion as to ***what to do..*** This is because if a territory is really unfamiliar and strange to oneself, there is no previous knowledge of having been there. ***It is natural to be awkward, disoriented and inept.*** Service is that activity of **meeting the needs of the environment.** For example, you can give yourself to articulating the quality and force of whatever state you're in **without having to understand these aspects.** Or you can mimic and learn from those there before you who have been serving that state long enough to have established a sense of their identity there. It is in this way that service preceeds identity and that in order to find oneself, a certain amount of time in service is required.

CONNECTING ESSENCES

Connecting essences is an effective technique for rituals involving multiple facets, networks and/or inter-related regions...i.e., the House Ritual as presented in the first level of work, **Initiations.** Connecting essences is the process of entering one zone (let's say DREAM) and exciting its essence in your body, then... moving into another area (let's say KNOWLEDGE) **bringing the DREAM essence with you.** Connecting these two essences in your body evokes a new essence of both combined: DREAM KNOWLEDGE. Connecting essences is a good way to intersect realms and locate diversified areas of mutuality and cross pollination. (The main thing to remember is wait for the essence to emerge strongly first before bringing it into another area and connecting them together.) To assure the integrity of this function, make sure and frequent the zones you wish to merge inside you, previously and separately. **Before mixing essences, experience each for themselves first, in other words.** Take time to assimilate and savor the new information of the essences you are mixing.

RITUAL DESIGN

Three Levels of Work

The RITUAL DESIGN section hereafter presents three levels of work: **1) INITIATIONS; 2) DARK RITES** ***(of the Soul)*** ; and **3) ILLUMINATIONS**...roughly paralleling Beginning, Intermediate and Advanced ritual practice. More advanced ritual designs tend to carry greater CHARGE , LIGHT and INFORMATION thus requiring a deeper integrity, self-responsibility and presence to proceed scrupulously. **The greater the** ***presence, commitment*** **and** ***energy*** **generated in the WARM-UP...the more appropriate it is to draw upon rituals evoking greater intensities.** ***Thus, the intensity matches the integrity.*** Group & Individual integrity levels can be detected during the ritual preparation phases to determine the rituals most likely to amplify *present-time dynamics.* The more grounded we are, the higher we fly...integrity seeks challenge...stability invites acceleration...***the quality of the preparation determines the nature of the rituals to follow.***

INITIATIONS: entry points for Self-Initiation and internal access; rituals requiring emotional surrender and identification with forces evoked; tasks for exciting **self-reference and definition**

DARK RITES (of the Soul): ceremonial encounters with the Shadow...fears, resistances and other blocks to self-acceptance; rituals for exposing undeveloped and neglected aspects of oneself towards their reclaimation; (recognizing and owning ones negative self-projections); rites for **testing endurance amidst intensities**

ILLUMINATIONS: rituals for release and transcendence from oneself (difficult, if not impossible, to gain entry without having previously passed through Dark Rites); tests for clarifying **form, quality and development of personal & collective myths; spiritual and planetary ceremonies**

ALL THE FOLLOWING RITUALS BEGIN AND END IN ***NO-FORM.*** *WHEN A RITUAL IS COMPLETE, PARTICIPANTS RETURN TO NO-FORM TO DISSOLVE IDENTIFICATION, SO THEY MAY PREPARE FOR THE NEXT RITUAL BY RE-ENTERING*

NO-FORM.

SAMPLE RITUAL SESSION

The following series of activities demonstrates a typical session in the medium of ritual theatre. The Physical Warm-up period remains the same for all sessions. It is suggested practice to enter some form of Polarization before entering actual Ritual Design, primarily for the purpose of emotional flexibility and self-catalyzation.

1) A setting is selected and a rare area established.
2) The ritual setting is sanctified.
3) A power spot is discovered and owned.
4) A little circle is constructed. (Preparation for Physical Warm-Up.)
5) Meditation. Spinal Flex. Stretch. Sweat.
6) A transitory run is selected. Return to the Little Circle.
7) A polarity is selected and executed alone. Transitory Run on your own.
8)Group circle. Feedback and brief, to-the-point comments.

Ritual #1

Set DEITY APPROACHES up (See INITIATIONS). After moving through the three approaches, jog around the periphery of the workspace integrating your insights. When you are done, meet in the center of the room for Group Circle.

Group Circle

This is a brief (3-5 minutes) checking in period for comments and questions in a non-judgmental atmosphere (See Group Circle).

Ritual #2

Set up floor plan for THE FIVE ELEMENTS (See INITIATIONS) with the intent of self-discovery, i.e., no group interaction. After having explored ALL FIVE ELEMENTS, return to NO-FORM outside the ritual arena. (playing time 20-30 minutes) Proceed to Transitory Run.

Transitory Run

While jogging, explore directional and non-directional modes for locating your point of balance. Vocalize the modes while you run.

Ritual #3

Each participant selects an ELEMENT to serve. (Some ELEMENTS may be paired up and others may be lacking altogether. If this expresses the true state of the group at this time, go with it. The dynamics will reveal the innate direction and shape of the group mind. In other words, there is no need to make it "perfect" or symmetrical if this is not innate to the group at this time.) Each participant enters NO-FORM outside that section designated to his/her ELEMENT. When all are in NO-FORM, participants enter their ELEMENT and absorb its influence without moving. When the ELEMENT compels movement, participants serve its expression into a **rhythm, song,** and **dance.** When their dance is strong enough to be challenged by interaction, they do so. The purpose here is in discovering **ones relationship to the Whole** through the various effects one has on others and how one is influenced by others **while remaining true to the source of ones power in the ELEMENT chosen.**

Integrate GESTURE to articulate the essence of this relationship to the Whole. Experiment with a series of GESTURES and pay attention to the myth and/or story developing. Follow everything to its natural conclusion. Tie up loose ends...**end cycles**...initiate beginnings this way. Be sensitive to the natural closure, so you don't have to force yourselves past it. After the ritual, everbody returns outside ofthe arena and enters NO-FORM.

Group Circle

Here, a group circle might be more mandatory for integrating and moving on. Keep it non-judgmental and expository...no need to rationalize and try to figure things out now. The main intent is reporting what happened. (After the group circle, participants may wish another ritual. If so, one can be constructed on the basis of the current needs of the moment. In advanced ritual theatre work, entire ritual sessions are constructed on the basis of individual offerings, usually emerging during the Warm-Up cycles, i.e., certain issues may emerge while working out physically that may wish further exploration. Rituals can be co-designed through combining more than one contact point (one suggested by each person) and/or from a series of rites evolving along a certain theme. Sessions can last anywhere from 2-4 hours, with three hours being the average. The Warm-Up cycles alone last about an hour.)

MUSIC

Live music is a powerful force. It is not suggested until the final ritual of each session and/or when it becomes obvious that the internal dependence of participants is strong enough to **not be broken.** ***Musicians take note: to evolve along the spirit of this work, it is important not to impose musical directions but accent and extend the energy expressed by those participating in the rituals.*** It may be of great help for musicians to also enter NO-FORM and locate the same contact points within themselves as the ritual participants have. This connects everyone to the same source and permits sonic cohesion. (Musical instruments that have worked effectively in the past are: PIANO, SYNTHESIZER,ELECTRIC GUITAR, CONGAS, PERCUSSION, FLUTE, and CHORUS.) **The intent of this work is in moving from an internal source.** Music is introduced to challenge the integrity of this intent and infuse another dimension, while serving to amplify the psychic atmospheres precipitated by ritual participants...

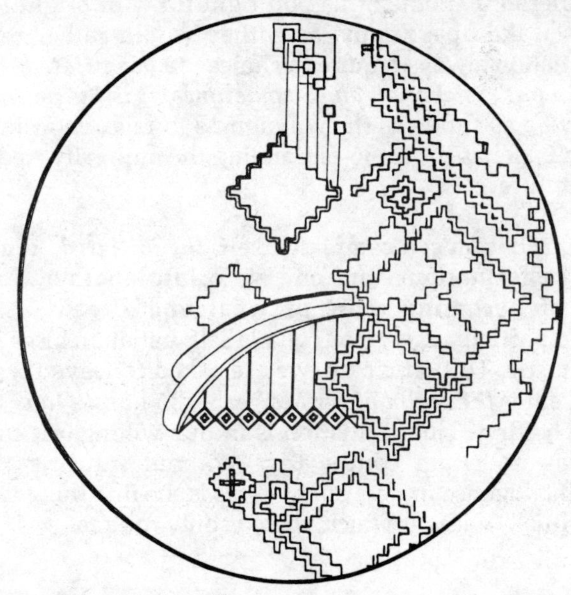

Initiations

THE INTERNAL LANDSCAPE

Every moment is an initiation for those living by the laws of their innate being. Gaining entry to the inner sanctum of the Self remains an enigmatic route until, through practice, one becomes more familiar with its spiraling path. Once one has found their way back and forth between the World and the Soul, it is **the bridge between them** which needs strengthening so as to assure our passage from one dimension into another. **Initiation is this interdimensional shift between "reality tunnels."** To exit one tunnel, our attachment to it must dissove before we are ushered into the next corridor. So, a certain surrender and/or sacrifice is required for each initiation or interdimensional shift. Without this willingness for internal surrender, the secret passageway is blocked by the locked doors of our attachments, resistances, and fears.

One of the greatest initiations humans are capable of is *waking up to themselves.* One form initiation takes is in our **creative response to the unknown.** A creative response is alive and real, unlike the mechanical, conditioned reactions we are also capable of. For example, fear is a common mechanical reaction to the unknown. Excitement could possibly refer us to a more creative response to this same unknown. Each human wakes up differently. Some of us pop right up with bright I's and bushy tales. Others wake up grumpy, as if they would rather remain in bed sleeping. Initiation always requires a **choice...*to be initiated, a direction is selected and a path is chosen and... sometimes, it is the path that chooses us.*** This may be as subtle as the willingness to relax choosing, which is a choice in itself...or...as dynamic as claiming the **authority** to determine the shape of your future.

Before an initiation can complete itself, *the initiated* must undergo a complete transformation from one state into another...including the conversion of becoming more of what one already is. Without a willingness to **participate** with our whole self, initiation loses initiative and turns mechanistic. To participate, we are asked to leave the realm of the Watcher and enter ***the realm of the Merger,* who knows how to be what it already is.** The first "true" Initiation is in our willingness to merge with **No-Form**, as no ritual comes alive without infusing the spark of Originating Intelligence into its intent. This is the first thing to know about "charging a ritual", without which, there is only routine.

CIRCLE OF NO-FORM

Either alone or in a group, enter the No-Form stance in the center of the ritual setting. Initiate the Cloud of Unknowing. Visualize or sense a circle around yourselves (on the floor below you) so that the Cloud(s) of Unknowing is contained. At the strongest point of No-Form, project the Force of the Earth outside of your central circle, so that this Force has a life of its own which fills the remaining area of the ritual space. When you are ready, from No-Form step over the border of your central circle and into the Force of the Earth. Discover how much you can give your body to the Earth. Discover your willingness to completely surrender to the Earth and be a vehicle for its expression...through sound, gesture & motion. When complete, return to the central circle and re-enter the Cloud of Unknowing.

TRUTH

Mark a circle and project What Is Most True (at this time and space) inside and after entering NO-FORM, step into the circle. Locate your point of service to this quality by creating space for its expression.

TOTAL ACCEPTANCE

Locate Contact Point with the quality of TOTAL ACCEPTANCE. After surrendering oneself to it, sanctify your space with this quality so that "all is permitted."

THE GOD OF YOUR HEART

Locate Contact Point with the God of Your Heart, serving Its expression into a gesture communicating Its essence. Then, begin a dialogue with the God of Your Heart...sound, motion, and gesture. Discover a new form of prayer in this interaction.

PATTERNS OF MOTION

From No-Form, locate Contact Point with "patterns of motion" emerging and passing through you. Serve these into expression. Go through cycles of patterns, letting them die and be reborn as new designs. Discover **movement as nourishment** as a method for inviting graceful endurance.

SHAPING

Locate contact point with "shapes" that come and go throughout your body. Like "patterns of motion," shaping goes through cycles and challenges our capacity to give our body over to these shapes. Find the shape that resonates closest to your innate sense of who you are.

DEITY APPROACHES

Project DEITY WITHIN to a specific area of the ritual setting. Project a path from No-Form to where the presence of the DEITY WITHIN resides. From NO-FORM, traverse this path and simply ***be in Its presence..*** Walk back to NO-FORM. Approach DEITY WITHIN again, with a question and be in Its presence ***with the question.*** Return to NO-FORM. Approach It again ***stating a need.*** Return to NO-FORM.

DREAMING FORMS

Designate one side of room to NO-FORM and the opposite side to FORM, with and equal size space between them dedicated to DREAM. From the potential state of NO-FORM, step into DREAM... the realm of many possibilities, as of yet, uncrystallized and incessantly changing. Pass through DREAM and follow one of these "possibilities" out into FORM, wherein this possibility immediately crystallizes into **Vivid, Specific Gesture** complete with its resonating sounds. **FORM is a high-tension zone where movement reaches its absoulte peak expression.** After absorbing its message, walk backward into DREAM... dissolving the form to re-enter the realm of possibilities. Then, back into NO-FORM. Repeat this cycle three times and go deeper each time *in all three dimensions.* When you are done, take the three gestures and connect them together as a series of tableaus while looking for the story/myth it tells.

SPINAL SLIDE

From NO-FORM, within the Little Circle, sense the spinal cord as one unfragmented pole... from its base and up into the skull. The top of the pole expresses the **clearest quality accessible** and the spine's base, the **densest quality accessible.** Discover how low you can **slide** your consciousness so it densifies. Then, slide up to the top to clarify awareness. Practice sliding up and down this spinal elevator challenging your capacity for owning Top and Bottom levels. Let your voice match their energy levels: resonate. The intent is with **creating more space within your being by stretching Top and Bottom apart...** hence, deepening your density and heightening clarity. In conjunction with the Spinal Elevator, select that level most appropriate to explore in-depth. Let this development include the entire body, so your whole self expresses that one level of consciousness.

THE TREE

Locate contact point with self as TREE. Sense Top and Bottom energy sources... the sun shining above, the earth absorbing below. Determine which source you need energy from to restore point of balance and give yourself over to it. Oscillate between the roots and the branches until you realize the whole tree within you.

EMOTIONAL ESSENCE

Stand in No-Form. Project an EMOTION behind you, letting it exist there in all its life and color. Invite it in through the back to fill your NO-FORM until it starts moving your body. While moving, begin paring away any arbitrary or exess motion to arrive at its essence. Resonate a sound...

GRAVITY/LEVITY

One side of the room is designated the HEAVIEST WEIGHT accessible; the opposite side, the LIGHTEST. The gradations in between articulate the transitions. Start from No-Form and enter THE HEAVIEST... moving towards the LIGHTEST. Pause in the center to check your balance. Move back and forth until both sides grow equal in valu:. POLARIZE.

VIBRATION

Same as GRAVITY/LEVITY... but replaced with the SLOWEST VIBRATION and the FASTEST VIBRATION accessible.

CREATOR-DESTROYER-NOURISHER

Mark a large triangle and in its center, an area dedicated to NO-FORM. (This ritual works exceedingly well with numbers divisible by **3.**) Project inside each corner an altar to serve as a focal point for the: CREATOR, DESTROYER & NOURISHER. From NO-FORM, approach the altar of the deity you need to devote yourself to for overall balance. Develop a **prayer, a chant and a dance of devotion** to that deity around its altar. Return to NO-FORM to disengage your loyalty and then, approach another deity, proceeding like before. Eventually, visit all three and then... start moving directly from one altar to another in a circular motion, passing through each **devotional tone** as you go. Return to NO-FORM.

THE FOUR SEASONS

Mark a large circle and quarter it, designating each fourth to a different season. Place AUTUMN & SPRING in opposition, as well as SUMMER & WINTER. Designate the area outside the Circle to NO-FORM. From NO-FORM, enter the Circle and traverse through them all until you can accelerate the pace of time, wherein you pass through many years or seasonal cycles..in a matter of moments.

THE CROSS

From No-Form, visualize a large CROSS above you. Draw it down and be in its center, where the two poles meet. Let it influence your whole being. Then, expand your being to fill the cross from the inside, so your soul takes the shape of a cross.

REINCARNATIONS

Delineate the room into 5 associated areas so the following dimensions are placed in a linear cyclic pattern: NO-FORM... BEING BORN... LIVING... DYING... AFTERLIFE... Participants begin in NO-FORM and enter BEING BORN. From here, they traverse into LIVING, and onto DYING. After DYING, they enter the space designated to AFTERLIFE... and thereafter walk back to the "Waiting Room" of NO-FORM to be born again. Go through as many reincarnational cycles as necessary. Watch for any connecting currents along the way between lifetimes. Be open to relating with others from whatever stage you're in.

THE FIVE ELEMENTS

Mark a large circle with a little circle as its center. Draw and quarter the whole circle. Designate elements of FIRE & WATER in opposing quarters and AIR & EARTH in opposition, as well. The central little circle is dedicated to the underlying, bonding force of AETHER. Designate the space outside the large circle as NO-FORM. From NO-FORM, enter one of the elements at random. Once inside, give yourself completely until the ***need emerges to enter the other elements, then, do so.*** Pass through the AETHER anytime you feel like it. Frequent all the elements. Recall which were more accessible, which were not. Return to NO-FORM. **Re-enter the circle to cultivate a deeper appreciation for the value of all five elements and the energetic functions of each.**

THE LAND OF LOVE AND FEAR

Start with a standing Group Circle in the center of setting with everyone facing away from center. While touching at the shoulders, everybody enters NO-FORM. All project a sphere of PURE LOVE 3-5 feet above the circle of NO-FORM. 5 feet in front of group is the periphery of a larger circle enclosing everybody. On the other side of this border is projected THE FEAR ZONE. **The intent is drawing down PURE LOVE from the sphere and bringing it down through the open crown and into the Heart Center where it generates itself.** When the generation of PURE LOVE is strong enough, participants resonate a sound to its power. This develops ***into a tone... a melody... a song.*** When participants are strong enough in their LOVE, they enter THE FEAR ZONE bringing their LOVE with them. If and when they lose touch with their LOVE and are overcome by FEAR, they find their way back to the center to regenerate their LOVE. The direction is with bringing LOVE into THE FEAR ZONE and detecting when it's time to return to LOVE again. The "HEARTSONG" developed earlier is a device for maintaining LOVE in THE FEAR ZONE.

THE PIT

Mark large circle with the intention of projecting **depth** into it, as in a ever-deepening pit. Then, project Creatures of the EARTH, WATER, FIRE or AIR down in there...letting them squirm, swim, crackle and fly about inside. In NO-FORM, walk around the pit's periphery sensing the activities brewing down around in the pit. After a revolution of NO-FORM, enter the pit and spiral down to its deep center to choose a creature to bring out. Choose the creature you believe has the most to teach you. Bring the creature out of the pit and into an area that you proceed to sanctify. Dialog with the creature to learn how to gain its allegiance, knowledge and favors. After you are complete, bring it down into the pit again and resolve the relationship. Move out of the pit and return to NO-FORM.

BODY OF LIGHT

From NO-FORM, project a sphere of GOLD, CHARACTERLESS ENERGY above your head. Draw down a beam into your crown, letting it fill you. ***Become the beam, so you catalyze your "light body"*** and let its essences move you around. Resonate a sound to match its quality. After development, project this internal "being of light" **outside your body** and dialog with it ***as an autonomous force.*** When you are complete, command the being of light to return to its source in the GOLD SPHERE above. Then, return to NO-FORM.

THE THREE TEMPLES

Designate three separate regions or rooms as Temples of the: HEAD, HEART and GUT. In a neutral zone, set up a group NO-FORM circle while standing. From NO-FORM, journey through each temple to surrender to its Point Of Worship (Head, Heart or Gut) and to form an altar in each as part of this process. After traversing through all three, return to the Temple you need to learn most about. Go there with the intention of apprenticing to its God by becoming a Priest(ess) of that Temple. Discover the rituals, songs, prayers and meditations appropriate to that Temple and serve the POW that makes these possible. When you feel strong enough, exit the Temple as the Priest(ess) bringing the power of that Temple with you and enter the previous neutral zone to interact with the other Priests and Priestesses. Whenever you lose touch with your Source, return to your Temple and renew your POW in order to return to the World of Interactions with your "religious power" restored.

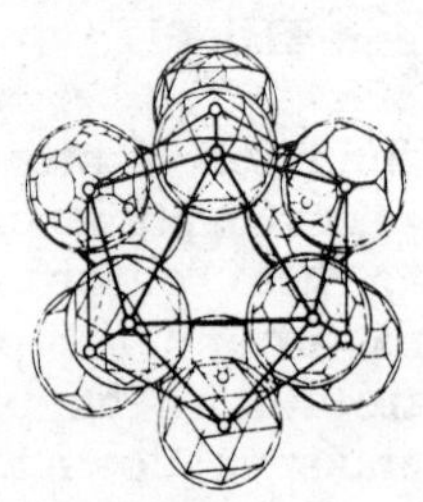

THE HOUSE RITUAL

Psychic psychologist Carl C. Jung often interpreted the symbol of a house in dreams as representative of the Self, with each room expressing specific internal compartments wherein particular aspects of the psyche chose to reside. Within the symbolic languages of both Tarot and Astrology, the metaphor of the house also comes into significant focus. In the Tarot, the card of the Magician is related to the second letter of the Hebrew alphabet "Beth" meaning... **house**. An astrological chart is divided into twelve wedges refering to specific areas of life activity and these areas are called *Houses*. There are, no doubt, countless other references to the house as symbolic of something else. This brief introduction will suffice to invite our participation in a ritual initiation using a real house **as its setting.**

The kind of house best suited for a House Ritual is one which has been made into *a home*. It helps to have at least four rooms available and, if possible, a backyard. Each of these rooms will maintain distinct functions and all will be associated towards the singular intent of procurring a certain kind of initiation rite... one wherein the everyday, mundane functions of each room are amplified to archetypal status. As each home is different, it will take careful observation and sensitivity to detect **the characteristic energetic of each room**, so as to form the basis of the ***name*** given to that area. For example, hallways between rooms might be assigned as NO-FORM ZONES. Living rooms could be named THE CHILD WITHIN, dens given to THE SHADOW, bedrooms to NOURISHER, the office... a TEMPLE. Once again, each house differs and the naming ought to ***synchronize*** with the innate feeling of each room and, extend this into a universal aspect.

One room should be almost completely cleared out of furniture while others can remain the way they naturally are. This will create a kind of polarity in the setting and support overall *charging* of the ritual. Rooms with furniture can be rearranged and certain props can be brought in to amplify evocation. However, all furniture should be designated symbolic and refering to a specific internal state or dimension, i.e., a couch is dedicated to the experience of SAFETY, so whenever anyone sits on it, they are permeated with this quality. A nearby chair could be designated as THE IMMOBILIZED SELF, providing opportunity for those who seek this facet of self-knowledge.

In other words, every mundane element is charged with symbolic significance and the entire house is transformed into a multi-dimensional chamber of magickal proportions. After the naming of all the rooms available to this ritual (and the hallways and transition points between rooms), we go into the backyard to decide upon its function. If there are paths, gardens, lawns... ***use them.*** They can all be designated as evolving phases along a singular unfolding journey. The wonderful thing about including a backyard is that its orientation is opposite to the house itself and brings another polarity into play. If there is a backyard available, it may be most effective to designate at least part of it to DEATH, DECAY or some form of TRANSFORMATION from one phase into another. This will leave the house itself open for ***re-integrating ones new self.***

Once the house and backyard have been re-named according to archetypal forces, it is important to meet as a group in the most open room... the one most minimally furnished. Here, a group circle convenes for meditation (possibly a Prayer Circle) and the introduction of ritual intent. The group then takes a walking tour through each room while the facilitator explains their various functions. (You may wish to place small signs over the doorways of each room to remind participants along their way.) After frequenting all the designated areas, participants should be led outside... preferably to a front porch which is designated as NO-FORM. At this point a brief physical warm-up is suggested. Anything from stretching out on the from lawn to several laps jogging around the block is appropriate or, ask participants to warm-up before arriving.

The ritual, as all the others, starts in NO-FORM out on the front porch and initiates itself with the entry through the front door and into the first room. Participants are encouraged to give themselves over to each room, hallway and phase along the sojourn of this House Ritual... and allow at least two hours for everyone to complete their cycles. Sometimes, depending on the house, this can take upwards of four hours or so.

After completion, participants should meet at the NO-FORM front porch where some kind of light food and drink is served. This is a good time to share the news of our initiation in the House Ritual. (As with every ritual, a good amount of time is required afterwards in NO-FORM.) For more advanced work in the House Ritual, see the ritual function of CONNECTING ESSENCES.

SAMPLE FLOOR PLAN FOR HOUSE RITUAL

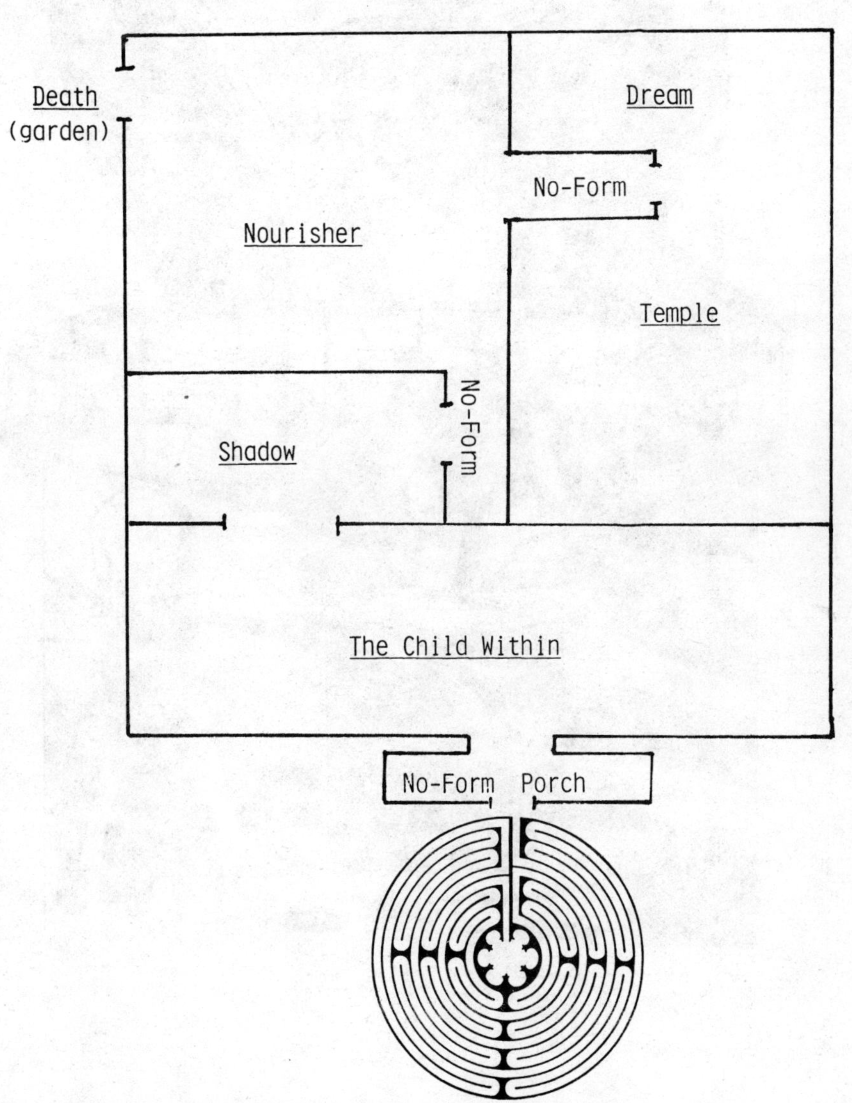

Dark Rites (of the Soul)

ENDURANCE

After gaining entry to the inner sanctum of Self via the previous Initiations section, a new level awaits those who are willing to test their commitment, integrity and endurance. Dark Rites open up **shadow-related** issues like personal fears, hates, resistances, frustrations, and otherwise neglected and thus, undeveloped areas within the Soul. These areas of self-denial are in need of attention, response and integration before any resemblence of the Soul comes to life **in the body.** A particular challenge to these Dark Rites seems to be with testing our capacity for **endurance in the midst of great intensity.** These are trials-by-fire. Whatever the fire does not harden, it will purge away...

Dark Rites are blessings in disguise... especially for those participants dangling on the precipice of discovering their own Shadow. Often we are immobilized by the sheer lack of expressive modes available to release these forces into conscious recognition. Dark Rites provide triggers and forms for accessing and expressing the Shadow. They enable the opportunity to face our fears and befriend ourselves until we are ready to embrace the Shadow itself. The bright side of the Shadow illuminates our lives with its enormous **vitality**, without which, we over-organize and die, spiritually. If it were not for chaos, evolution would not be possible at all. The truer the chaos, the truer the emerging form. Dark Rites prepare us for Illuminations by helping us cultivate an appreciation for chaos, without which, clarity of form could never develop.

Our Shadow aspects are but distortions of our true qualities; inherently, there is no spilt between our defects and our qualities. As we come to recognize and accept our defects, we can see them transform and convert into the qualities of our innate being...our particular "element." Dark Rites are especially ***healing*** to individuals with out-of-control, ego-inflating tendencies. Or those **phases** everybody goes through, on occasion, where we deny anything "bad", "wrong", "evil" and/or "stupid" about ourselves. In these phases, we tend to blame others for those undesirable traits we refuse to accept in ourselves. This demonstrates one way the powerful "psychic projection" mechanism loses control. The ritual function of PROJECTION is a method for regaining command of what is innately a psychic ability...a capacity for "charging" an object (talismans) or space (Rare Area) with our own energy (also called "ego-state cathexis"). Dark Rites help us become aware of our projections and as a result, develop the psychic muscle for doing it **consciously.** This, in turn, prepares our entry into Illuminations of advanced ritual work, where little or no projection is necessary at all.

DEATH

Project DEATH into a designated area at least ten feet from self. From NO-FORM, walk into its territory and surrender to its influence. Bring this to a gesture communicating its essence and return to original area of NO-FORM. Return to DEATH again, this time locating your CONTACT POINT WITH *RESPONSE TO DEATH.* Develop relationship with DEATH. Return to NO-FORM area.

DR. DEATH AND THE WARRIOR

Ritual duet. Each individual prepares alone in their Little Circles. One has Contact Point with DEATH PERSONIFIED and the other, WARRIOR. The WARRIOR develops a *song, rhythm and dance* in his/her Little Circle, while DEATH PERSONIFIED tunes into WARRIOR. When each is strong enough in their integrity, they leave their Little Circles and enter a specified arena of interaction. Ritual intent is for these two forces to meet and interact while remaining true to their respective Contact Points. DEATH carries the power of touch and can terminate WARRIOR with it. WARRIOR has only his/her song, rhythm and dance expressinghis/her **will to live.** DEATH determines the end of the ritual by either touching WARRIOR or refraining thus, granting life extension.

CHAMBER OF DEMIGODS

From the NO-FORM stance, project a vertical tube/column of neutral energy running from above and down through your body and into the planet below. The top of the chamber opens up to ANGELIC KINGDOM and the bottom, DEMONIC DOMAIN. Angels fly up above as demons squirm and shout from below. Let angels fall down through the chamber and demons bubble up from below. One at a time, select one of each to BE & EXPRESS, then send back to their sources. These are aspects of Oneself.

THE IMMOBILIZATION MYTH

Project Immobilization Myth (how and where you are stuck, fixed and crucified) into an area at least 15 feet away. Visualize tunnel or hallway connecting you to this circle. From NO-FORM, walk through its passage and into the circle to embody the myth, **whatever it is.** Give time for its development and then, project an altar area within this circle and dedicate it to DISTILLATION. Upon approaching the altar, let the myth distill itself so you are left with its essence. Resonate a sound with this quality and its shape. Give yourself over to full-body gesture as a statue expressing your Immobilization Myth.

MOST FEARED THING

Project MOST FEARED THING into an area ten feet in front of self. From NO-FORM, enter the circle while bringing with you the element of SACRIFICE as an ally: the act of sacrificing an aspect of self in order to meet and respond to the MOST FEARED THING. Develop into a dance and song. (You may not have to sacrifice anything. It is there in case you need to.)

THE BLACK BOX

Designate an area of the ritual setting to RESISTANCE and project into its region, a BLACK BOX containing "that which is most valued". Journey into and throughout the RESISTANCE searching for THE BLACK BOX. Upon finding it, open it up. Then,relate to the RESISTANCE with what you found inside. When done, place the "most valued" back into the BLACK BOX and return it to its place in the circle. Exit the circle to NO-FORM.

THE BROKEN SELF

Mark a circle (this can be your Little Circle). Project BROKEN SELF or BROKENESS into circle. Enter the circle, surrendering to the influence therein. Develop the material through sounds, gestures, words, phrases and an eventual monologue to narrate and transmit the Myth of the Broken Person. Return to No-Form.

THE DANGEROUS WORLD

Cultivate Little Circle for optimum safety, comfort and vulnerability. Sanctify its space for maximum trust and permission to be yourself. Stabilize its four corners and develop their energetic functions. When complete, designate all the space outside your Little Circle as the DANGEROUS WORLD. When you feel safe enough to take risks, step outside and explore its territory knowing anytime you can return to regenerate safety in the Little Circle. If there are other people, designate them as CHARACTERS in the DANGEROUS WORLD. The intent is with sustaining your integrity and restoring your safety amidst the dangerous.

NIGHTMARE

Mark large circle. PROJECT reality of NIGHTMARE inside. In the circle's center, visualize and project a vertical beam of GOLD ENERGY. First, enter the circle to explore NIGHTMARE...being under its effect, while personifying its forces. After development of NIGHTMARE, relate to the GOLD BEAM from NIGHTMARE. Dialogue with BEAM. Then, thirdly, step into the GOLD BEAM...bringing NIGHTMARE with you. Let GOLD BEAM influence NIGHTMARE. Return through NIGHTMARE and back to NO-FORM.

EMOTIONAL TRINITY

Form a triangular space, designating each corner to one of the following: SAVIOUR, PERSECUTOR, VICTIM. The center of the triangle is dedicated to NO-FORM. From NO-FORM, move out and explore each corner and surrender to its influuence, letting yourself be shaped by the forces towards developing a character who speaks, gestures and walks like a VICTIM, SAVIOUR or PERSECUTOR. Make sure and visit all three points on the trinity before returning to NO-FORM.

THE DIVINE COMEDY

Create large triangle as ritual floor plan. Designate each side to the following internal states: HELL, PURGATORY, HEAVEN. From NO-FORM, travel along each side moving through each state...as a group or by yourself. If there's a group, place everybody inside the triangle except the traveler. The group functions as Greek Chorus, providing sounds and movements to intensify the traveler's experience of each dimension. The points of the triangle are dedicated to NO-FORM. When the traveler makes it to one, everbody enters NO-FORM until the traveler moves into the next state.

THE JOURNEY

Create a large circle that is also a spiral. Designate the outer periphery to SUPERFICIAL- SURFACE SELF and the central area as the DEEP -CORE SELF. The entire spiral is THE SELF with all the gradations between the Surface and the Core interlaced with "blocks"and resistances. Start at the SURFACE area in No-Form and begin spiraling towardsTHE CORE . Find the "blocks" along the way...work through/around them. When arriving at the CORE , let its quality determine what follows.

SUFFER, DROP AND DIE

Select aspect of Self you wish to sacrifice. From NO-FORM, let this "self" stand five feet behind you in all of its life and color. Then, invite it in and let it SUFFER, DROP AND DIE as a movement inside you. If appropriate, conduct a funeral for the old dead self. If it happens, reincarnate.

PIECE OF RESISTANCE

Into the Little Circle, project RESISTANCE, refering to whatever subconscious resistance is occuring. Enter the circle and become the resistance until it forms your character. *Personify resistance.* Live it out and if possible, exorcise "the entity of resistance" from your body and relate with it. Send it to the Earth to be re-possessed. Return to NO-FORM.

HEALING CEREMONY

Locate contact point with body part in dis-ease. Give yourself over to the virus or whatever it is. Then, after developing it as a character/energy, disengage from it for the purpose of dialoging. Find out what it feeds on. If you are ready, command it to leave by radiating your innate energy.

ANGELS IN HELL

In your Little Circle, project ANGELIC KINGDOM..."the natural habitat of the angelic self." Enter Little Circle and make yourself at home in Heaven. Designate everything outside your Little Circle as HELL then, find someway to fall out of your Circle and into HELL. Explore HELL while sustaining your Contact Point with the ANGELIC KINGDOM. Find a way to return to the ANGELIC KINGDOM.

DEMONS IN HEAVEN

Same as ANGELS IN HELL but you start out by evoking the DEMONIC DOMAIN, making yourself at home as a DEMON IN HELL. Somehow, get pulled into HEAVEN (that space outside your Little Circle) then, explore HEAVEN sustaining your DEMONIC INTEGRITY. If you are ***converted*** while visiting HEAVEN, return to your Little Circle and reclaim the DEMONIC DOMAIN ***in HEAVEN's name.***

ANGELS AND DEMONS

Group Ritual. Divide room in half...one side is HEAVEN, the home of ANGELS...the other side, HELL, the home of DEMONS. Participants are divided so equal numbers inhabit both domains. Each side takes time to develop its own individual identities (as DEMONS or ANGELS), then each side explores activities to bond with their respective clan. (ANGELS bond with other ANGELS, DEMONS with other DEMONS.) When both groups are stabilized, they approach each other physically and respond, while remaining loyal to their source. Let whatever responses unfold as DEMONS and ANGELS interact on each other's territories.

THE ANIMA/ANIMUS CIRCLE

This is a solo ceremony based in the Jungian psychological model of the **anima** (& animus) suggesting that within every man, there lives an autonomous and intensely erotic feminine force responsible for inspired creativity and sexuality. In women, it's called the **animus...**a self-organizing, rational masculine spirit wielding high-focused, creative and discerning powers. Besides projecting the defects of our Shadow onto others, we also tend to project the anima/animus onto whatever external woman/man most closely replicates the feeling/appearance of our inner source of creativity, or Soul/Spirit. This often occurs during the experience commonly known as Falling In Love (Read **Fatal Romantics** of CHAPEL PERILOUS in *ANGEL TECH* by the author; Falcon Press). Of special concern here is when High-Flying Romance elicits the visceral response of being Souless & Emotionally Vacant during the absence of The Beloved. **Who is The Beloved ?!?**

The intent behind this ritual is primarily three-fold: **1) To invite** The Beloved into conscious recognition as the Anima/Animus **2) To establish** an ongoing rapport and relationship with Her/Him and **3) To learn** how to magnetize members of the opposite sex to ourselves due to a renewed relationship with that aspect **in oneself.** In other words, once a man can associate with the Feminine Within, real-live women instinctively detect this and are drawn to the possibility of **a real relationship.** The same goes for the Woman/Animus rapport. (Since the sexual orientation of the author is decidedly hetero, no mention will be made as to how bisexual/homosexuality works in respect to this model.) This ritual is rather potent in its capacity for attracting more men and/or women into your life via the psychic recognition it excites. *Consider yourself forewarned.*

The ANIMA/ANIMUS CIRCLE is suggested to whomever is willing to manifest its three-fold intent. It is also very useful to those who have ended up in CHAPEL PERILOUS as a result of losing their Soul and/or having fallen under the spell of an **Anima Attack.** Men and women are **possessed** by their respective Anima/Animus in different ways. The Anima attacks the man when he has neglected to **express his feelings as his own and thus, succumbs to "moodiness" of epic proportions.** The Animus slays the woman when she neglects to **control her own mind and is driven to controlling externals in a non-stop pattern of self-denial.** This kind of possession can be dispersed once the Anima/Animus is related with directly instead of indirectly, by our identification with it. (It's hard to **relate** to someone when you're too busy **being** him/her.) The ANIMA/ANIMUS CIRCLE ritual has two parts:

THE RITUAL

Part One: After a thorough preparation, mark a circle and sanctify its space. Stand outside the circle while facing it and enter NO-FORM. Project everything you innately know to be the AN!MA or ANIMUS (hereafter refered to as ANI) into the circle. (You may have to "call ANI back" from wherever s/he was last projected) From NO-FORM, enter the circle and feel/sense ANI there. Let ANI enter you from whatever point in your body and/or aura **s/he desires.** Let ANI fill you and start devoting yourself to him/her. Surrender to ANI's influence and invite him/her to possess you. (Make a **conscious choice** for this to occur so you know what it feels like). Give yourself over to **becoming** ANI by letting ANI shape and determine each passing moment. Create time for development then, crystallize the essence of your devotion to ANI in a gesture while resonating a sound/tune/song to match this "crystal."

Part Two: Exit the circle and return to NO-FORM. Spend enough time neutralizing whatever charge ANI instilled...the deeper the NO-FORM, the freer you'll be. When ready, enter the circle again and repeat Part One until you are devotional again. Then, project ANI **out of your body** while in the circle and, start relating to him/her. **Establish rapport.** In the relationship that ensues, find out what NAME s/he wishes to be called and what **s/he does best. Do this by asking direct questions.** Once you know these two things, refer to ANI by name and command ANI to do what s/he does best. Discover what function ANI plays in your psyche and what your role or position is in relation to this. Test your new-found knowledge through applied experimentation. When you figure it out and have had enough, exit the circle after resolving with ANI. Return to a deep NO-FORM.

The Living Funeral

Resurrection Ceremonies

A **Living Funeral is any ritual enactment or ceremony formalizing emotional and/or psychological death for the purpose of self-renewal.** It can be as simple as a 10-minute solo polarization to a 4-hour group effort with elaborate prepatory phases. The primary intent behind a Living Funeral is **creating the space and permission to die and be reborn.** How this is actualized, depends on the individuals present, their ritual knowledge and willingness to be responsible for generating and sustaining the "power field" most conducive to its unfolding. The following ritual tasks are excerpted from previously executed Living Funerals for those wishing to form a basis for constructing new versions.

1) The group sits in a large circle with at least 3 feet of space between individuals. Everybody takes turns talking about personal experiences with any form of death. Then, everyone is asked to **re-name** death with a term(s) communicating the essence of their personal experience.

2) **HIT THE DIRT...**A Children's Game. One person is chosen as The Executioner and everyone else are !ntentional Victims. The Executioner stands in the center of a large circle made up of the others. Loud rock'n'roll or marching music (Joy Division has worked well) starts the circle of Intentional Victims moving. When one of them is ready to die, he/she *catches the attention* of the Executioner and communicates his/her fantasy: how she/he wishes to die and/or be killed. The Executioner, in turn, recreates the setting and if needed, the characters to fulfill this

destiny. During the fantasy enactment, the others stop and watch. They are also available to the Executioner if he/she requires more players to complete the scene. When done, the circle continues until another Victim steps forth. All take their turn...then all fulfill *the Executioner's fantasy.*

3) **WHAT I DON'T WANT TO BE WHEN I GROW UP...**Another Children's Game. Each participant takes turns presenting a characterization to the rest of the group in a spotlight situation. This character is the direct expression of the title of this task. Care should be taken to be as honest as possible and to relate by eye-contact with the others during your time under the spotlight.

4) **SECRETS...**a confessional exercise. Participants individually approach other members and whisper a personal secret about themselves to the other. This secret can relate to present-time fears and/or feelings we have towards others in the room or things we haven't told anyone before about our personal history. **The intent here is with building trust.** Living Funerals require deeper sanctification due to the kind of vulnerability necessary for true transformation. Without a good deal of trust and safety, this ritual runs a high risk of being contrived and, ineffective.

5) **THE TWO CHAIRS.** A circle of Paired Chairs...Each participant has a pair of chairs and these pairs encircle the setting. One chair is designated The Seat of the EGO and the other, The Seat of the SELF. From NO-FORM, one sits in the EGO CHAIR first and gives over to its perspective. Then, when complete, one enters NO-FORM and sits in the CHAIR OF SELF. The task is alternating chairs so one becomes acquainted with each perspective and the manner by which they **CAST JUDGMENT.**

6) **JUDGEMENT DAY**. Two participants start out sitting in two chairs, one in the SEAT OF EGO and the other in the SEAT OF SELF. The rest of the others await about twenty feet away clustered together in NO-FORM. The person in the SEAT OF EGO calls a name by random while the person in the SEAT OF SELF simply beckons that person forward from NO-FORM. The person called now stands facing the seated two while the EGO casts its judgment on that person. When done, the SELF casts its judgement. The person then sits in the EGO CHAIR, while that person moves to the SELF CHAIR and the previous SELF joins the others in the NO-FORM group cluster. The process repeats itself with the EGO calling a name at random. (It might be appropriate to have the SELF signal the EGO when it is ready to start the next cycle. Take your time to locate contact points with EGO and SELF.)

7) **INVOKING THE DYING SELF.** Participants lay down in rows, much like cemetary plots are arranged. While lying on their backs, they all enter NO-FORM and Project **That Part Of Me Which Is Dying or THE DYING SELF, six feet below.** Let it exist down there in all its fading life and character. When you are empty & hollow enough, invite the DYING SELF up to enter your body from behind, filling you with its presence. Begin resonating a sound to match its energy. Through development, let this sound become a word which is the NAME of the DYING SELF. While this is happening, project the STATE OF AFTERLIFE above you and let it develop **on its own.** Chant the name to send THE DYING SELF up and out of the body and into the STATE OR REALM OF THE AFTERLIFE. Chant the name until THE DYING SELF is gone and absorbed into the realm above...then stop chanting. **Be with your death.**

8) After completing the previous INVOCATION and having been with your death, project the surrounding area as THE WAITING ROOM or LIMBO or the name best describing **TRANSITION BETWEEN REALMS.** When you feel ready, rise and move into this zone. If encountering others do so as if you are all waiting together. You are...

9) After exploring LIMBO (#8), participants search the area within the boundaries of the WAITING ROOM/LIMBO area for "void spots" where the feeling of NOTHINGNESS is strongest. Into these areas, project a CHAMBER OF NO-FORM. Enter the chamber and merge with NO-FORM. From here, locate your contact point with your **NEW SELF.** Let NEW SELF flood the chamber and determine all direction. Resonate sounds and with development, evolve a NAME for the NEW SELF. Chant the name.

10) **INVOKING THE NEW SELF.** Participants take turns laying on the floor while others stand overhead, quietly chanting the name of THE NEW SELF. Chant the name in as many different intonations as possible. Meanwhile, the person whose name is chanted lies on his/her back taking it all in and responding. Everybody takes turns.

Due to the high degree of vulnerability required for this ritual to actually work, it is absolutely essential that the Rare Area be deeply sanctified and void of any outside interruptions whatsoever. The use of incense, candles, drapes, music, scripture and other environmental enhancers have also contributed greatly to the atmospheric intent of this ceremony.

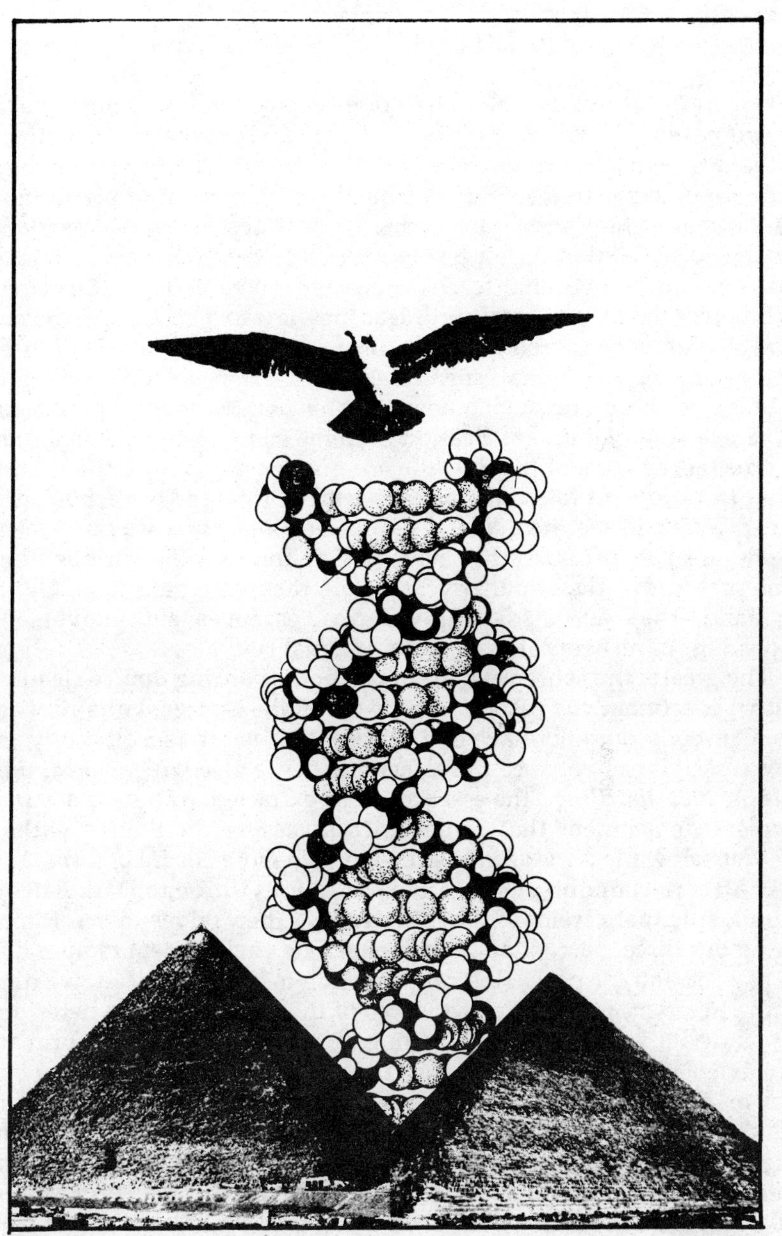

Illuminations
CLARITY OF FORMS

The primordial phases of ritual involve internal surrender to an all-encompassing, enveloping stage of self-discovery. It is essential to relax the desire to control how it will look and instead, simply submerge into the total, subjective side of personal experience. This preliminary phase, no matter how indulgent and sloppy, is absolutely necessary for catalyzing Self-Initiation. After being exposed to the undeniable effects of self-penetration, we become ready to advance in the work. **Advanced ritual involves the diligent process of learning how to *distill* from the raw, vulnerable first stage...seed essences, forms and movements.** Within the bubbling mix of emotional surrender there exists specific energetic directions and structures which emerge ***after they have cooked enough.*** From here, a kind of **disidentification** from the energies evoked is needed to become more **aware of them, *while not disengaging completely.*** There is a shift from content ***to*** form, in that we are learning to extract essences from expression to see the material of our creation. In a way, the forms emerging are part of us, as they have passed through the various filters and internal gridworks of our psyche before their emergent state. On the other hand, they are also simply forms, essences and movements developed in the alchemical oven of our internal laboratory.

The greater the sense we have of our bodies during Source relations and ritual enactment, the easier it'll be to detect the emergent qualities and forms. Our body does not have to disappear. If we can feel our body as a hollow vessel, it can enhance the alchemical sense of ***mixing, containing, dissolving and distilling*** the essences to be extracted. There is a certain benevolent detachment that comes with accessing the Source without losing yourself while serving its expression with more ***clarity of form.***

After re-claiming our negative projections (through Dark Rites of the Soul), spiritual ceremonies begin availing themselves to us. Rituals engaging our direct perception of the immediate environment require little or no psychic and/or psychological projection to work. Instead, we draw upon the inherent, geomantic properties of the setting itself to determine the ritual designs. This can be anything from the way shadows form and play in an enclosed room to the natural boundaries and zones created by a stream or gully outside. With enough sensitivity, participants and the rituals themselves draw upon ***forces and qualities already present in the setting to motivate the ceremonies at hand.*** These are spiritual rituals as they are based upon **what is sensed** rather than imagined, projected or postulated. The latter are tools for accessing oneself and bridges to cross towards self-transcendence.

BODY GEOGRAPHY

From NO-FORM, locate contact point with Body As The World...complete with its internal geography and climates: deserts, jungles, mountains, valleys, swamps, grasslands, oceans, lakes and rivers. Select that area of the world you wish to explore and locate your contact point there. Find a way to adapt so you can live there.

THE TRAVELLER

Begin BODY GEOGRAPHY. Once you locate a region to live in, take what you need to travel throughout the regions. Give yourself the attribute of changing form as a way of adapting to the various locations.

PROGRESSIVE ESCAPE

Locate contact point with What Is Real. Enter it through the intent of Escaping **Into** Reality. Find its center and pass through to the other side.

DREAM CHARACTERS

Designate a specific area to DREAM. From NO-FORM, enter DREAM with the intention of developing a character from its essences. Evolve this until the character comes to complete fruition and dies. Let it die and be reborn/reincarnated as another character. Follow through as many cycles as necessary to feel complete.

AWAKENING

Designate area as That Part of Self Which Is ASLEEP. From NO-FORM, enter this area and surrender to its influence. Work with DEVELOPMENT until the SLEEP converts to DREAM...and the DREAM converts to AWAKENING.

COLORS

Divide setting into six related areas. Project a color into each so there is an evolution: RED, ORANGE, YELLOW, GREEN, BLUE and VIOLET. From NO-FORM, move between these colors. Locate the colors you resist the most. Return to them and surrender to their influence.

THE ONE COLOR

From NO-FORM, enter an area designated for the projection of your most difficult color. Let this area cover three phases or shades of that color, from its pastel to its medium and its darker hues. Explore the shades as a way of coming to terms with the color.

CLOAK OF COLOR

From NO-FORM, locate contact point with one color. After exploration and development, wrap its opposite color around you while sustaining the original internal color. Relate to other(s) while maintaining both colors.

THE HUMAN SYSTEMS

From NO-FORM, locate contact point with SKELETAL SYSTEM as a whole and let all movement originate from here. On other occasions, replace SKELETAL SYSTEM with the CENTRAL NERVOUS SYSTEM, DIGESTIVE SYSTEM, MUSCULAR SYSTEM, ENDOCRINE SYSTEM, REPRODUCTIVE SYSTEM, RESPIRATORY SYSTEM...exploring the LIMITS of each and expressing their innate rhythms.

HUMAN QUATERNITY

Divide setting into four inter-related areas. Project the essences of FEELING, THOUGHT, UNDERSTANDING and WILL into these. Explore each to discover the current state of your internal condition. Determine which you require more of to maintain true development and balance, and move there.

SACRED FLAME

From NO-FORM, locate contact point with SACRED FLAME WITHIN. Surrender to FLAME, identify with it and BE THE FLAME. After development, disengage from FLAME and locate contact point with GUARD to THE FLAME. (Let FLAME continue as an autonomous force in your space while you establish relationship with it as THE GUARD to FLAME.) After development of relationship, **merge** GUARD and FLAME together to form THE GUARDIAN. Develop a dance of THE GUARDIAN.

THE CLOUD

From NO-FORM, locate contact point with Self as VAPOR. Develop and let this condense into CLOUD. Stay with development required to condense further still...increasing moisture, density and weight. Develop this until you are RAINING. Proceed with whatever follows.

CREATIVE DESTRUCTION

Draw a large circle, then a circle half its size in its center. In the smaller, center circle project PERPETUAL CREATION OF STRUCTURE and the outer circle, PERPETUAL DESTRUCTION OF STRUCTURE. Move between realms until each becomes intolerable by itself and compels the need for its opposite.

GRAVITY

From NO-FORM, locate contact point with GRAVITY AS SOURCE OF ENERGY. Give yourself to this source and develop rapport with THE EARTH through it. Let this relationship develop a dance and a song. Incorporate Gesture.

THE GARDEN

From NO-FORM, locate contact point with MOST FERTILE SOIL. After surrendering to its density, fecundity and moisture...become aware of the SUN above you. Let a SEED DROP FROM THE CENTER OF THE SUN down into the soil. Stay with SEED as a contact point. After some development, let it RAIN. Let the SEED sprout and break the soil's surface. Feel yourself as the SEED AND THE SOIL. Let the sprout deepen its ROOTS while growing towards the SUN. Let the plant develop into WHATEVER SPECIES OF FLORA IT IS. If it bears FRUIT, let it ripen and drop to the SOIL breaking open, rotting and going to seed.

CORRIDOR OF LIFE

Designate a long, narrow strip of space with a small circle at each end. In one circle project CREATURE and in the other, SPIRIT. From NO-FORM, begin by entering the SPIRIT circle. After surrendering to SPIRIT, begin by walking into CORRIDOR OF LIFE (the narrow strip between the two circles). With every step, SPIRIT densifies and moves closer to CREATURE.

Feel the gradations along the way and be sensitive to the midpoint. Once reaching the CREATURE circle, enter it and surrender to its influence. When complete, begin the journey back to SPIRIT along the CORRIDOR OF LIFE. Move back and forth between CREATURE and SPIRIT until a relationship is developed and expressed through GESTURE and SOUND.

ENTERING THE UNKNOWN

Mark a large circle and divide it in half. Designate one side to THE KNOWN or WHATEVER CAN BE NAMED, and the other side to the NAMELESS UNKNOWN. From NO-FORM, enter the KNOWN. Clean it up and develop a personal sense of ORDER there. Select items from your life that are Most Important to you and arrange them in THE KNOWN as properties. (These items can be possessions, ideas, feelings, people, groups, etc.) When complete, move to the border between KNOWN and UNKNOWN and stand there sensing the UNKNOWN before you. When ready, enter the UNKNOWN and be influenced by its mystery. When it's time, return to THE KNOWN and discover its relation to THE UNKNOWN. Are the items selected still of importance? Do they need to be rearranged? If so, re-order them to reflect the existence of THE UNKNOWN. Fortify the boundaries of the KNOWN, as well. Then, when complete, enter THE UNKNOWN again. Return to THE KNOWN and refine the ordering process to reflect THE UNKNOWN.

POSITIVE-NEGATIVE-NEUTRAL

Divide the setting in half, projecting POSITIVE on one side and NEGATIVE to the other. Let the dividing line serrve as the CORRIDER OF NO-FORM. Enter the side which exerts the greatest "pull". Travel between sides, letting the TRAVELLER become NEUTRAL ENERGY. Sustain neutrality while containing the forces of POSITIVE and NEGATIVE within you as you visit their respective regions.

ASTRO-DRAMA

part #1

Divide circle into 12 wedges designating each to a different House. From NO-FORM, travel from the 11th House cusp into the 11th House and proceed through the 12th and into the 1st and so forth, until you reach the Midheaven. At the Midheaven, come to a GESTURE crystallizing the essence of your evolution. (This works most effectively by superimposing your own astrological house placements according to your birth chart.)

part #2
Repeat part #1 but project the Planets' placements into the ritual floor plan of the Houses and enter from the 11th House again. Relate to the planets as specific FORCES which activate once you've entered the House its in. After moving through all the Houses, move to the center of the circle and sense the planetary positions around you and their relationships.

part #3
Select a major aspect. If there's an opposition, set up a POLARIZATION ritual. If there's a square, include resistance into the ritual. If there's a conjunction, locate your contact point with its synthesis.

part #4
Locate the placement and sign SATURN is in. Combining information from HOUSE, SIGN and SATURN itself...develop a ritual to articulate and dramatize its role in your chart and your life. Play SATURN yourself. Project SATURN outside of self. Experiment.

THE TAROT

Extract the cards of the Major Arcana into a pile. Select, at random, one card. From NO-FORM, locate your contact point with the archetype symbolized in this card. Through DEVELOPMENT, discover its myth and story as it evolves into a character. Incorporate the colors of the card as your internal environment. Return to a big NO-FORM.

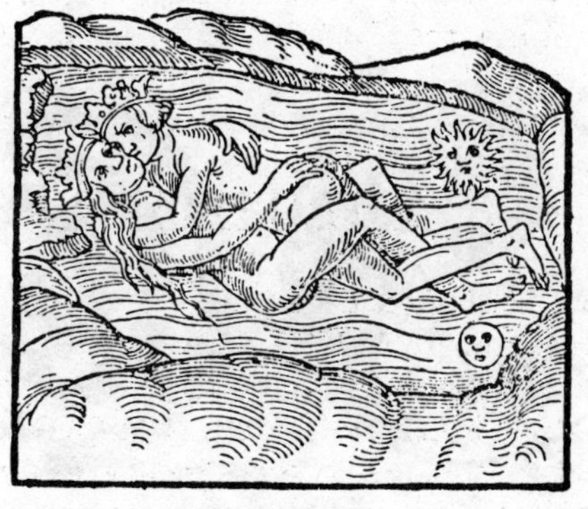

THE YIN/YANG CIRCLE

A Group Ritual for Men & Women. A small, centrally located circle is designated to the **YIN** force and a larger circle (enveloping the smaller one), to the **YANG** force. To start the ceremony, the women gather together inside the inner YIN circle and the men position themselves around the periphery of the outer YANG circle. Everybody enters NO-FORM simultaneously. The women begin receiving the YIN force and start resonating sounds to herald its presence. **The men remain silent.** While maintaining their sonic resonance, the women begin giving themselves to movement while following the direction the YIN force wishes to rotate. **The men remain still.** Once all the women are following the same direction of rotation, their circle starts turning in that direction. The men then begin resonating sounds and **initiating movement** of their circle in **the opposite direction of the inner circle.**

The two circles are rotating in opposite directions. During these contrary rotations, the YIN & YANG circles start relating with each other *while maintaining their respective integrity via sound, movement and gesture.* Develop these interactions so the YIN/YANG relationship clarifies and grows more and more obvious. Stay with it regardless of exhaustion, wherein it is suggested that you adjust your energetic output to accomodate your pace. Find a natural conclusion.

PART TWO: Reverse procedures for men and women...Men move to the YIN circle and women, to the YANG circle. Repeat the ceremony as before and crystallize the conclusion in gestures and/or group statues or forms to communicate the essence of the relationship.

EARTH SURRENDER RITES

Planetary Helixing for Men and Women

The Earth is a living, breathing entity that has chosen to incarnate as this planet. Human beings inhabiting the surface of the Earth are engaged in a reciprocal feeding process with the planetary entity. Amidst the possibilities inherent to human interaction, there exists a certain kind of man-woman relationship serving to generate bio-psychic energies for feeding the planet. Not every man or woman is meant to function in this capacity. Through a series of synchronized events, planetary intelligence arranges for certain men and women to meet for the ritual function of its feeding. Who these men and women are, and how they serve the planet is a primary concern for the understanding and practice of Earth Surrender Rites.

Within each human being, there lives a "genetic conduit" for absorbing, integrating, and transmitting signals from the DNA matrix. Besides articulating the genetic blueprint of Life As We Know It here on Earth, DNA is also the native language of the planetary entity. The DNA code is binary in structure as its signals traverse between polarities to generate and maintain Life Itself. Humans developing internal resonance with DNA surrender to planetary intelligence and become conduits for its absorbtion, integration, and transmission. The man-woman relationship required for Earth Surrender Rites is **not** based on personal gratification or the mutual romance of personalities but the possibility of becoming instrumental to planetary feeding. Through cultivating profound states of receptivity, men and women learn to detect genetic/generic patterns of being... those which are innate to the bio-psychic structures maintaining our lives.

When the planetary entity coordinates meetings with a certain man and a certain woman to feed itself, there is excited an *intensity* that is not emotional in origin yet the emotions may react to it. This intensity is electromagnetic in nature and generates between the genetic conduits previously awakened in a man and a woman. There is an all-encompasing, self-enveloping quality to this intensity. It may have the effect of exciting tension in the physical body until the body knows what to do with the energy. This quality will release the **depth-feeling of infinity** shared between the man and woman as time dissolves and spiritual presence expands. A certain freedom of being or mutual autonomy tends to accompany the intensity, as well.

From a psychic perspective, humans are bio-electromagnetic batteries and the planet is a geo-electromagnetic battery. Humans recharge theirs by distinguishing and assimilating polarity within themselves. The purpose of setting up internal polarities is igniting an oscillation of consciousness between them towards the construction of an energetic source, or star. This process of polarization births a third "transcendent" quality which feeds the genetic conduit. This third point beyond polarity is pure, or generic, consciousness and its expansion is expressed as the intensity felt between a man and a woman in Earth Surrender Rites. When two energetic sources, or stars, generate more consciousness between them we have a "stellar polarity" forming the larger generator from which the planetary food is produced.

When the intensity between a man and a woman reaches "unbearable proportions", the planetary food is cooked and needs to be sent down to the Earth's core by the man. Genetically, man is more of a container as his inner essence is more feminine and so, provides boundaries for the ritual. It is up to him to make sure the container does not break from excess pressure from the electromagnetic power. The man learns about timing. Good timing happens when both man and woman are left with their integrity intact. Poor timing occurs if one or both human batteries are short-circuited and/or over-amped.

The woman's ritual function is with feeding the man *while he feeds the planet*. As he directs the power to the Earth's core, the woman connects her Heart Center to his with a beam of Earth energy. The woman's inner essence is more masculine, so she serves as the contained by drawing up Earth energy into her body and sending it to the man through her heart. This can be accomplished by connecting the inhale with pulling earth energy up through the base of her spine and circulating this energy throughout her body on the exhale. The repetition of this breathing cycle tends to stabilize the overall electromagnetic flux as it lends the energy a more manageable feel. (See GROUNDING CIRCLES)

This description of Earth Surrender Rites did not include possible psychological and emotional reactions to the shared intensity but instead presented the underlying structure of the process. Earth Surrender Rites, as described here, are not accessible to every man and woman and so, ought not to be contrived to suit the curiosity of friends and lovers. The set-up occurs by planetary arrangement whereby a man and woman are brought together by the power of intensity oscillating between their genetic conduits. Sometimes, emotional and psychological reactions emerge in relation to this kind of intensity which often obscure the true purpose of the meeting. Human culture has seeded human minds with images to help contain and direct tremendous forces towards socially accepted conventions. For example, perhaps the intensity between two human batteries is misjudged for human love and they enter the social convention of marriage. Planetary food is then fed to a more horizontal need emphasizing the fusion of the two batteries rather than their mutual service and recognition of the third node of the circuit, namely, the planetary entity itself.

In the midst of great intensity between a man and woman, it is often easy to identify ones emotional/psychological reactions with the power generated between genetic conduits and thus remain deluded about the possible true origin of that intensity. It is quite possible that a man and woman are brought together for the sole purpose of feeding the planet and very little else. They may meet on special occasions to work the ceremony and then, part ways until the next time. Equally possible is that a man and woman engaged in Earth Surrender Rites may share other activities together, as well. However, if a man and woman start out feeding the planet and then enter other areas of energetic fusion together only to discover their capacity to feed the planet diminishing, then it becomes self-evident what is happening. As the power leaves a certain couple, it undoubtedly travels towards magnetizing another man and woman together to accomplish the task. This power is **autonomous**... lighting and leaving on a moments notice, spiraling into its most direct expression.

Earth Surrender Rites is simply a name for one variation of many, many possibilities in the field of bio-psychic interactions between human beings and the planetary entity. The technology, design and basic blueprint for this ceremony was distilled from essences experienced by the author and reflect his bias, conceptual framework and Central Nervous System as it works to integrate this input.

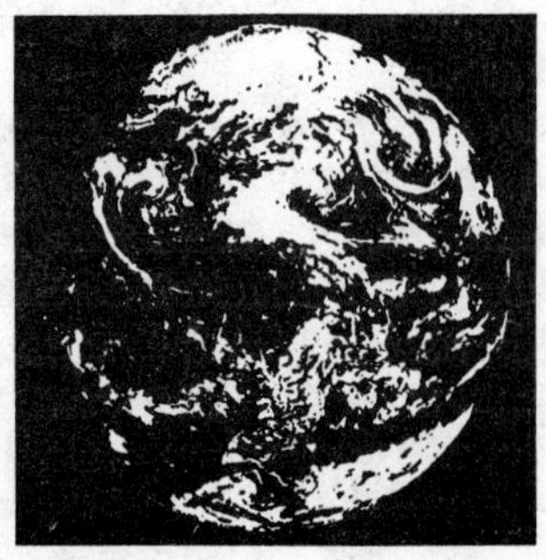

The man is a cottage
And the woman is a tree beside the door.

The man is a cottage
And the woman is a tree beside the door.
The man is a rock in a boulder field
And the woman is snow, melting.

He worships beauty
And wants to make all good things fruitful.
She is the daughter of Spoon Woman.
Her lap is fragrant and soft as tundra.

Spoon Woman lives forever,
Growing younger and older, older and younger.
He is learning to dig a pit,
And pour blood into it, and weep.

When Spoon Woman is older
Her face is like bark
And her hair is where the river has eaten its bank away
Leaving matted and tangled roots.

When Spoon Woman is younger
She is vanilla
And a newly washed cotton nightgown,
Sweet from drying in the sun.

He is the Son of the One Who Starts Things Up.
Jumped by the Grizzly Man,
Meeting the Dream Man,
He carves stone arrowheads
And makes pictures in the sand.

Talk to the stars now.
She says: Mother, Grandmother.
He says: Father, Grandfather.

When the man and the woman meet
Each one asks:
"What sound is this person today ?"

Today he is the song of the barn swallow
And she is soft rain weaving a sash on the pond.
Tonight
He is the sound of a coyote's paw digging in snow,
She is the sound of an acorn sprout
Pushing through the damp earth.

In their bed
The two of them sleep
Curled about each other.
And that spiral
Winds through the whole world.

CHRIS HOFFMAN
is a published poet seeking experimental expressions for his work.
He can be reached at: 6525 Kalua Road in Boulder, COLORADO 80301

GROUNDING CIRCLES & DREAMTIME RITUALS

by Antero Alli

The Grounding Circle requires two or more people to work. One person can practice its preparation and benefit yet the circuit completes itself with another(s). To arrive at the awareness of being a planetary node or "conduit", we must first pass through a Concept Free Zone and enter the Realm of Our Senses. The purpose of Grounding Circles rests in the **stabilization** of individual and collective energy fields.

If with a group of three, sit in a triangle; four, a square; five, a pentagram; six, a hexagon (6-pointed star). Any more, form a circle and any less, sit across from one another. Without touching anyone anywhere, close your eyes and center. Settle your awareness to the base of the spine so gravity collects there and feels like an anchor. Then, open the base of your spine. If your feet are flat on the ground, open your arches up. Get a sense of being **a dark, hollow shell** with these openings at the bottom. Watch your breathing and let it be natural, so you do not hold your breath. Then, connect your breath to EARTH ENERGY. On the inhale, **breathe in** EARTH ENERGY up through the spine's base and/or the arches and on the exhale, **circulate** this EARTH ENERGY throughout your entire body. Repeat this cycle of connected energetic breathing, filling yourself with EARTH ENERGY. This type of energy may start feeling "dense". Keep circulating it to discover your **capacity for permitting density.** How dense can you get? (EARTH ENERGY may create a sense of being more compact. This is because it is a natural stabilizer.) If you wish to increase the flow, breathe deeper while dilating the openings where you are drawing it up from. To decrease the flow, implement the reverse procedure. You are looking for your point of Maximum Density without losing consciousness.

Now, be sensitive to being a "bump on the planet." This is called Bump Consciousness and starts your nodal awareness. Feel that you are a protuberance of the planet itself. There is no difference between yourself and the planet. Be receptive to its vast support and strength. Then be aware (with eyes closed) of the other "bumps" around you resonating their transmissions of EARTH ENERGY. (if you're in a circle, sense a "ring of bumps." Let your body be influenced and moved by the EARTH ENERGY. How much can you give your body over to the EARTH? Feel free to tremble, shake and quiver. These are natural biological responses to a **resonant phase shift...**an acceleration of energy to synchronize with a higher level than before.

When you are ready to move on, place your arms out in front of you with your palms faced up (arms can rest on lap). While you are maintaining the cycle of connected breath, exhale excess EARTH ENERGY out your arms and through your hands and fingertips. Then, begin resonating a sound that **matches the frequency of the EARTH ENERGY.** (It matters **not** how it sounds but that you remain true to your contact with your source in EARTH ENERGY.) There's no need to control the sound or create melody. Instead, let the EARTH ENERGY determine the tone, pitch, key, and sonic direction. The only thing you need to do is resonate a sound to match the energy itself.

When you feel strong enough to link up with the other bumps, extend your right hand (FACED DOWN) to the person on your right and your left hand (FACED UP) to the person on your left. Keep cycling EARTH ENERGY through your body and out your hands. The intent in the link-up is to circulate EARTH ENERGY throughout the collective, while continuing the process of cycling it through yourself. There are **two** hand positions for linking up: 1) **with a gap,** and 2) **without a gap.** Experiment to feel what it's like to circulate EARTH ENERGY without physically touching the hands of others but passing the EARTH ENERGY through the gap between your hand and theirs. Then, close the gap by holding hands to feel what that is like. Alternate between the two positions for optimal circulation of EARTH ENERGIES.

Circulate EARTH ENERGIES until you feel complete, then withdraw your hands and renew your singular nodal connection. If you start to jerk or tremble throughout the GROUNDING CIRCLE, give yourself permission to acquiesce to these adjustments. Your body has its own ways of entering higher frequencies and deeper bondings. It needs to express itself freely to feel safe enough to continue. After every body has withdrawn to their own individual integrity conduits, send the excess Earth Energy to the core of the planet. The Grounding Circle is an effective preparation rite for ceremonies evoking a lot of charge, light and/or psychic energy. That's why it's called a **Grounding Circle.**

DREAMTIME RITUALS

When we go to sleep, we dream. Sometimes, we enter dreams as an observor; other times, as participants. It is through **dream participation** that we come to identify with our "dreamself" and explore the multidimensional dreamtime. *Now consider this:* Upon waking from your dreams the next morning, you are being **dreamed into existance** by this dreamself after **it** has gone to sleep in the dreamtime. ***Is it possible that we are either dreaming and/or being dreamed ?*** Is there only the activity of DREAM as the Buddha tells us ? Dreaming Rituals are those ceremonies revealing the bridge between the dreamtime and the waking daydream we call "reality." A dreaming ritual amplifies the contact points between our Daily Personality and the Deep Self of the Soul realms for the purpose of exposing their interaction. How can we trigger the **essences** of dreamtime into conscious recognition? By creating an outlet for their direct expression **through our physical bodies** as movement, sound, gesture and ritual enactment.

This is a **highly kinetic, non-interpretive** approach to dreamwork. It involves piecing dream remnants together to form movement cycles capable of exciting dream memory into present-time consciousness. The non-interpretive approach helps minimize the projection of our own symbolic meanings and/or imposed beliefs in exchange for becoming receptive to **the inherent meaning of the dream itself.** The intent of this ritual is at least two-fold: 1) **Emotional surrender; 2) Spiritual constancy** from participating with the intersecting realms of dreamtime **and** daytime.

To start the process, go to sleep with the intention of watching for and/or remembering a *movement* in your dream. This movement should stand out for its kinetic property, in other words... **not** because it means anything but because for some reason, it sticks out **as a movement** per se. You are not searching for meanings at all. When you awaken the next morning, immediately practice the movement as accurately as possible. The power of this ritual depends upon the degree by which the dream movement can be reproduced precisely, so, only execute those motions you are physically capable of. Run through it mechanically...casually, without any other intent than its kinetic execution.

Your "dreaming task" is in practicing this movement throughout the day by stopping to intentionally do so...perhaps three to six times before you go to sleep again. This weaves the dreamtime and daytime together by conscious execution of the dreaming task . Your objective is to accumulate

three movements from dreams. Practice them throughout one day or take three days to do it. They don't have to be from the same dream, or they can. They can be movements you saw somebody else do in your dream or something else...like a tree or a fish.

Once you have **three separate movements**, you are ready to construct a movement cycle. Before this, however,construct a Rare Area, Sanctify the Space, and Warm-Up to ready yourself. (See RITUAL PREPARATION) After warming up, practice each movement separately three or four times through each. You should be able to run through each one **with eyes closed.** The intent here is building a **kinetic memory** of each movement, so your body has become familiar with each one of them. Then join movement #3 to #1 by stitching the former to the latter somehow creating one extended motion, rather than two separate ones. Practice this eyes closed until you get it. Then, stitch this extended movement to #2 in the same manner, eyes closed. Then, move through to #3, eyes closed. You are now ready to execute **the complete movement cycle...**#3 to #1 to #2 to #3 to #1, etc. Practice this cycle until its repetition articulates specific rhythmic patterns. Do it with your eyes closed. Establish a kinetic memory of this movement cycle.

Part Two: Charging the Dreaming Ritual

If you haven't already done so, draw a circle on the ground either mentally or literally, with a stick or rock. Let it be at least ten feet in diameter. Step outside this circle and enter it with the intent of sanctifying its space. Then exit the circle and face it. Enter a NO-FORM state (See No-Form, RITUAL PREPARATIONS) and project (See Projection, RITUAL PREPS) the kinetic memory of your dreaming movement cycle into the circle **with all of its associations with the dreamtime** which originated these movements in the first place.

When you feel empty and receptive enough, enter the circle and let the first movement's ***energy structure*** fill your body and begin moving it into the physical form of that movement. Let this transition into movement #2, then on into the whole movement cycle. Feel free to move as slowly as you like to remain true to the energy structures of these movements as well as their dreamtime associations. Imagistic and emotional impressions may emerge as dream memory floods consciousness. **Stay with the movement cycle.** Don't stop to figure anything out and/or think about meanings. **Simply keep moving.** As you continue along with the movement cycle, be sensitive to any story or **myth** that may emerge. Let the myth unfold its message and let its energetic **penetrate into your heart.** Let it touch you, in other words. Keep moving through the cycle until the myth is so vivid and the feeling so strong that there's no place else to go but to culminate in a gesture communicating the essence of this moment. Briefly absorb the mythic intent penetrating your heart/soul/body and then, step outside the circle and re-enter a deep No-Form state to help neutralize the charge and bring you **back into present time.** If it's useful, write your dream down and/or speak about the experience with others. If possible, refrain from projecting any meaning into the results. Instead, discover the inherent message the Higher Self is relaying through the Dreamtime to you.

THE LAW COMES FROM THE MOUNTAIN

An Interview with Guboo Ted Thomas Chief Aboriginal Elder of the Yuin Tribe

In his youth, Guboo Ted Thomas was selected from 3,500 Aboriginal tribal members to inherit the position of chief elder of the Yuin in Australia. After outliving five young brides, three years ago the 78-year old Guboo chose to travel around the world teaching principles of the Dreamtime...the sacred heart of Aboriginal spirituality. Guboo says Dreaming develops the mind for long-distance telepathy and other powers that have become the norm for Aboriginal living. Guboo played a dijeridoo, (a traditional Aboriginal instrument made from the trunk of a certain tree that had been hollowed out by termites beforehand) before we spoke while he was visiting here in Boulder, COLORADO, April 28 1987 to show color slides of Australian power spots. The interview followed a rather participatory path as Guboo insisted I stop asking him questions so I could read him stories written by himself. I've not included these stories as they were clearly meant for those present at that time. You had to be there, in other words...

Antero Alli: Tell me about yourself.

Guboo Ted Thomas: My name is Guboo Ted Thomas. Guboo is my tribal name and Guboo means "good friend." So, today, I am your good friend. As I look back in Dreamtime and see Australia, it is a land of dreaming where the law comes from the mountain. Here, the Aboriginal people have roamed around the bush for 50,000 years...listening to the birds, animals, Mother Earth... and She teaches us to send messages by our minds... hundreds of miles to our people. Up in the mountain is the place to talk to the Great Spirit, who we call **Darama.** And Darama saw that the Aboriginal people were in tune with the Mother Earth and blessed them. There has been no war on Australian soil. This is why the Dreamtime is so important to us...it is always bringing us together.

AA: Is there a way to speak about the Dreamtime, Guboo ?

GTT: Yes...there is a way...and then, maybe not. Dreamtime is a very important tool for our people. Dreaming is the main way we use the mind, you see. It starts outdoors in a very quiet place where there is no noise and where the wind is blowing. Here, all around are Nature Spirits. You have them around here, too. Not where you have cleared the land...the spirits go back to the trees then, to the woods and wait there. In Australia, we take you to the outback and sit you down where I put red ochre on your forehead. This means respect, like the red band I wear on my head when I travel here in America. Then, I would talk to you and be in the spirit of the land and bring that spirit here (gestures to interviewer's heart). After walking in the woods for some time, you would dream and spirits would visit your vision. Yes, you would see these spirits and they talk with you. People today know that something's going to happen, that the world is going to change but we've never changed with it, we're still back where we first started. The dreaming is a way to be in the change of this world...and Australia is the last land on Earth that has the dreaming.

AA: Are there ways you help others enter the Dreaming ?

GTT: We need a spiritual cleanout first. Fasting on grapes for two days will bring you more power, so will praying and meditating. We have Dreaming Camps where we take people to the mountain...sometimes small groups, other times a few hundred. One thing you must know. You come as a child and learn how to crawl before you walk. I know today you have your education but I don't want you like that. I want you to come the way I want you to come...as a little child. Take every step. So, if you've got an education, you've missed two or three steps. Listen what I say...how do you touch a tree and feel the love of that tree ? Sometimes, you have to blindfold people and let them find their way around the rocks to learn. The rocks there are like natural churches...altars, so we don't need no artificial churches, you see. Just stand by the rock circles on the mountain and speak to the Great Spirit. You will feel a vibration...you will hear Darama, the Creator. Your words must come from the heart or it's just blah blah blah...this you must learn before Dreaming.

AA: What kind of tools do you use in your work ?

GTT: We have stone implements. We make our own knives, tomahawks, and that. The Aboriginal people were stone masons long, long ago...50,000 years...tempering the stone so they could hit the hard wood without breaking their tools. We know how much power is needed and where to hit the tree to chop it down. Anytime we take something from the Mother Earth, we pray to her first. We make killer boomerangs from wood and hunt kangaroo. Before we hunt the kangaroo, we pray to its spirit and to the Mother Earth. You know...the Aboriginal people were once very tall...seven foot tall...big, powerful men. Look at us today...I'm only five foot six. Since we've been eating white man's food, I'm getting smaller.

So, you see the difference ? The Aboriginal food was blessed and had vitamins. It was good for you. I think the Aboriginal people were better off then, than they are today... There are not as many trees today. The trees are always two together, a male and female...that's creation, you see. You separate them and what happens ? We've lost love for the trees. "Wapoo" means **beautiful bush**, or tree. I have these clapping sticks which I've made from a prayer to wapoo and I sing to wapoo when I play the sticks. I sing now. I know if you or the people don't listen to me sing, the birds and animals and the trees will hear. (Pausing first...Guboo sings, while playing his clapping sticks. After his song, Guboo smiles and continues talking)

Wapoo. The Aboriginal Sunrise Ceremonies are very special to our people. It starts when the sky is black, beautiful black. When the sun's yellow circle arrives, it turns the sky red. This is why the Aboriginal flag is half red, half black with a yellow circle in the middle. At the Sunrise Ceremony, I meditate and ask the Great Spirit for direction. My hands fill with electricity. I touch you and you feel it, too. I heal people this way...my Grandmother did that, too. I learned all about that when I was a young fellow. Umbarra, the Black Duck, is the special totem of our tribe, the Yuin. We learn to respect the elders who hand on the Law. The elders guard the Law and the Law guards the people. This is the Law that comes from the mountain.

AA: What do you see in the future ?

GTT: I remember, one time ago, a lot of professors gathered to talk about the world and the problems we're having today. One bloke got up and he said, "I think we should ask the Aboriginal people what went wrong." They would not lower themselves to come and ask an Aboriginal what went wrong. Man don't take notice what Aboriginal people say because we've been here over 50,000 years and what do you think that means ? (pausing) It means they mine the Uranium out of the ground and the green ants, they leave. When the green ants leave for good, the Dreaming goes with them. In February 1988, I am going to Ulura where there's an Aboriginal Sacred Site...a power point called Ayers Rock. Here, I'm getting 6,000 people together to link hands and connect with the rest of the world through the dreaming. We can tune into Findhorn, Tibet, America, Africa, the whole world from this place. Everyone is welcome to come. Everyone is welcome to link up then... wherever they are in the world. This is how the Dreamtime is.

VOCAL CREATIONS

A Basis for Sonic Resonance

The following sonic meditations are designed to enhance the natural voice as a resonating instrument for expressing the Self in ritual work. These vocal exercises aim at meeting three specific objectives: 1) **FLEXIBILITY** of the voice; 2) **EXTENSION** of sound throughout the whole body; and 3) **COMMUNICATION OF UNITY** from integrating three primary "centers" called: HEAD, HEART and GUT.

Three fundamental tools are now presented as a bridge for the fullfillment of the previous objectives. They are:

1) **RELAXATION**: recognizing ones "point of strain" while vocalizing and diminishing its force when this occurs. There is no reason why the voice needs to be constricted when a gradual, gentle development can effectively expand pitch, tone, power and color. Relaxation **expands** the voice.

2) **BREATHING**: sound "rides" out on the breath and serves to energize the instrument and increase lung capacity. The breath is so fundamental that you should be able to breathe through the soles of your feet. Breath **supports** the voice.

3) **INTUITION**: the source of sound is silence. Cultivating intimacy with silence is essential to the "motivated sound", one with a life of its own. From the silence of NO-FORM, we are influenced by a force or aspect of our nature and this can be expressed through vocal resonance. Intuition **connects** the voice.

The following "sound cycles" can be practiced alone and/or in a group. If they are expressed collectively, it is important to emphasize the need for self-commitment and the internal concentration to vocalize ones own source **while others are doing the same.** This practice can aid in the discovery of ones own vocal limitations. Before entering the exercises, it is suggested practice to warm-up physically, emotionally & vocally for at least 15 minutes prior.

SOUND CYCLE #1 (standing or sitting spine erect) "HOMING"

1) Breathe the letter "H". Gradually voice it from wherever it emerges most naturally in your body. Now, locate the lowest region in your body it can resonate from, i.e., your belly, pubic bone, base of your spine. From the lowest point, vocalize/breathe the letter "H".

2) Add the sound "OH" to make the sound "HO". Repeat the sound "HO", starting at your lowest point and raising it as you voice the "O", i.e., start the "H" in your belly and let the "O" bring the "HO" up to your lungs. So the "HO" starts in your belly and ends up in your lungs. Repeat.

3) Add the sound of "MMM" to make "HHHOHMMM". Start the "HHH" in your belly and raise it to your lungs with "OH" and up into your nasal area with the sound "HHHOHMMM". Repeat several times. Now just practice the "MMM" sound in the nasal region until it "buzzes" or tickles there.

4) Add an "invisible E" sound to make the word, "HOME". Repeat step #3 and add the "E" after the nasal vibration stage by sending it (the E) out the top of your head and into space. Watch this "E" disappear into the void. Start the whole process over again. "HHH" in the belly...rasing it to lungs with "HHHOH," then up to nasal area with "HHHOHMMM", then send that silent "E" out the crown and into space.

The previous sonic meditation serves as an ACCELERATOR and can be used whenever our overall energy requires either breaking up and/or raising. After HOMING, you may want to bend over (letting your head bow and hang) to release any excess energy. The acceleration may elicit light-headedness so, re-stabilize yourself.

SOUND CYCLE #2 (standing) Masculine/Feminine Polarization

1) From NO-FORM, locate contact point with MASCULINE. Use the letter "H" followed by any long vowel (HAY, HEE, HOO, HO, HI) to vocalize MASCULINE. Bring a kind of "primitive breath" into play and move MASCULINE down into your belly if it's not already there. Primitive breath is fiery, sudden and short. Repeat the "H" sound with vowel.

2) Send the sound and energy from the gut down through the legs and into the earth. Use the "H" sound to do this. Then alternate with the various long vowels: HAY! HEE! HOO! HI! HO! emphasizing focused breath and directional, controlled movement. Locate the rhythm of these repeating sounds and follow through. Make this a statement of determined and controlled effort. (See Directional Movement)

3) Return to NO-FORM, then let FEMININE drift down from above your head into your crown. Without controlling this force, serve its expression as a "hollow reed". Let it sway your body, especially the arms, hands, and fingers. Start resonating a sound which matches this energetic direction.

4) At will, return to MASCULINE and HAY, HOO, HO, HI, HEE. Then, at will, return to the FEMININE by relaxing the self-determined and highly controlled MASCULINE grip. Alternate between both locating your point of flexibility between the primitive breath of controlling your voice (MASCULINE) and letting your intuition guide you (FEMININE).

Emphasize the three tools of RELAXATION, BREATHING and INTUITION. There is no need to strain the voice at all. Be easy in the transition point between MASCULINE and FEMININE, as there is a natural shift and conversion there which requires no forcing. Return to NO-FORM.

SOUND CYCLE #3 (sitting or standing) The Breaking Point

1) Discover your lowest pitch without straining...use all three tools to stabilize your lowest note. Do the same by finding your highest pitch. Repeat both, one at a time, until they audibly expand your range.

2) Now, discover how long you can sustain both pitches without strain. Once again, use the tools of relaxation, breathing and intuition.

3) Start with your lowest pitch and SLIDE up to your highest pitch...gradually and gently. SLIDE from your highest to your lowest. While sliding up and down between each pitch, locate your "breaking point" whereby the continuity of sound is broken. Keep sliding until you know exactly where it is.

4) Focus on the vocal range before and after the break. Flip back and forth between them with the break separating the sound there. Flip back and forth between both sides of your break to fine tune exactly what pitch your break expresses.

5) Invent or develop a sound to express the pitch of the break so the sound bridges the gap. Relax into this new sound. Slide up and down to test its resiliancy.

THE VOICE AS ARTIST

An Interview with Paul Oertel

By Antero Alli

This meeting with the internationally-acclaimed voice artist, Paul Oertel, took place September 5th, 1986 in his studio in Boulder, Colorado. Onstage since he was ten years old, Paul's extensive theatrical/dance/voice background also incorporates the study of human anatomy. Since 1970, he has co-created with his wife, Nancy Spanier, in a series of Inter-Media Performance pieces featured throughout the U.S.A. and Europe.

ANTERO ALLI: Speak about the value of relating to silence and how this relationship influences the quality of sound.

PAUL OERTEL: The foundations of my initial work came from Kristin Linklater, an acting/voice teacher at the NYU School of the Arts in NYC. The bottom line to establishing vocal technique was finding that point of no effort. We started with lying on our backs and observing breath until the breath was not being motivated by any noise whatsoever. Even if the mind continued creating noise, the actual breath was silent. This created one open channel, so that no matter how tense I am...this channel would not be interfered by my neurotic habits...physical, emotional and psychic tension. **The breath itself will produce communication in silence without effort.**

AA: When you work one-to-one with someone, what do you look for first to find out the most about them?

PO: What usually happens first is that there's some sense of the individual's gift and their need. That usually glimmers forth when they walk in the room. Then, after that it's mostly a puzzle. What are the overlays, misconceptions, pretensions, and blocks that made it difficult for the person to access their gift? Then come the exercises to create the experiences for breaking up the blocks and confusions...to make it certain to the person that those things are not necessary.

AA: Touch upon the conversion point between sound into movement and dance.

PO: You can sometimes use sound to unblock the issues and sometimes movement and you can play back and forth depending on where the person is most open. If the person is blocked in the physical body and they have a fairly open vocal channel, you can hook in that way. What we usually find most difficult in voice class is the value judgment **about the resistance...**

AA: ...the resistance of the resistance...

PO: Absolutely. So, if the person says they feel like an ugly, stubborn, stupid donkey, then if we begin to dance out this ugly, stubborn, stupid donkey we discover that the individual without value judgment has a wonderful time.

AA: How can one vocalize intense feeling without blowing people away? And is there a way to contain expression without diluting its power?

PO: That's a very important question. My experience is that it has to do with the relationship between space, flesh and emotional flow. For example, if a person is expressing heightened anger and their flesh is caught in it and they are totally invested in it as if that is their identity, it tears up the body...**exhausts and debilitates the person.** It may produce a kind of catharsis but it wipes them out and they may have to go home and sleep. It pollutes the space and they don't get much insight from the experience because they have no perspective or point of view. Therefore, what to do?

In the body, we found that if the emotional flow is moving up the front of the spine but the person feels quiet and completely safe behind it then you can let anything fly and it will flow right out through an open channel out the body. The person is sitting there watching it with enough perspective that this other phenomena doesn't happen. Anatomically, we can go into the back ribs, so the person begins to feel: "Oh, there is space back there". And as they separate that space, they begin to experience the emotion in front of the space. Then they can actually sob and not feel frightened because they are **behind the emotion and not in it.**

AA: Let's go back to the issue of containing expression without diluting its power...

PO: It was put to me very well by an acting teacher named Olympia DeCaucous, a Greek woman in New York, and she said there was three things you can do with an emotion. You can stuff it, you can throw it out, or **you can experience it in your flesh.** Of course, the "stuffing of emotion" produces neurosis and sickness. Throwing it out often leaves somebody devastated...someone who gets the energy. But if you take the energy and actually put it into your flesh...pour it through like a sieve, then instead of having the emotion go to the world, **it goes through the muscles.** In that process, it becomes refined, filtered and this produces insight which creates understanding. In the audience, this works because it lets them handle the heat.

AA: What is resonance and how does it happen?

PO: Anytime you have a space closed off or muscles that are tight, it's like filling a violin with cotton or a room with pillows. As the muscles are freed, that area then will resonate. Another thing that is interesting is that places in a person's body that will not resonate have no consciousness. **Often, awareness is enough.** One can point to an area in the body and by becoming more aware of the spot, its resonance will increase. So, it turns out that one can develop a whole vocal technique that is based purely on awareness...where the more aware of your physical being you become, the more your voice opens up. **The flesh is really the barometer.** If you look at the flesh and it's becoming open, freer, lovelier...you know something is working. If the flesh is getting tighter, tenser, hardened, shortening and space is being lost...you know it's not working. Often times people will sacrifice their intuition for a certain effect that may be more sociologically or politically acceptable. **If a person learns to trust their instincts, they arrive at breath, relaxation and intuition...as well as their own personal aesthetic, integrity and individuality. They can arrive at their innate gift and ability to be of service and of use relative to their role on the planet.**

AA: How do you help people get beyond their concepts and closer to their own instincts?

PO: **It has to be by an experience rather than an argument.** An experience has to be created that is so sensuous, so pleasurable...so wonderful and undeniably real that they don't want the other thing anymore. They make the choice. I help the experience happen. If one experience doesn't work, then others are made. I have tried to argue people down and it's futile. The mind is infinitely clever. Who am I to tell anybody what to think anyways? It's none of my business.

AA: How can the voice become more flexible and sensitive to conveying the subtleties of the human heart's song?

PO: **It's a question of removing fear.** As the fear is removed, the human heart's song appears. As the tensions, preconceptions and notions are removed...it's like a bird in a cage singing with all kinds of locks, cotton, mufflers and stuff around it. The whole time the bird is singing yet the person can't hear it and no one can hear it because it's all buffered. Gradually, the person starts to hear it and asks, "Is that me? Am I that beautiful?".

AA: Talk about singing with the whole body...

PO: **If a part of the body is blocked or denied, it won't have awareness.** As we spoke earlier, where there's no awareness there's no resonance and expression. Let's say a person feels a vibration in the head and then the emotion moves down to the buttock seeking expresion...the voice wants to drop down into there. If this person has a belt of tension through their diaphragm, then the energy drops down and hits the diaphragm and the person suddenly feels nauseous...the expression doesn't happen. So, it's a question of making all the tracks free and all the dams so the water can flow freely everywhere. **It's the removing of the blocks so that the whole thing can work. There's nothing to be done or created; the creation is already there.** The whole body would work instantly if there was nothing dividing it into fragments.

AA: How do you neutralize and dissipate the charge that often accumulates while performing? What do you do after the show? How do you let it go?

PO: That, of course, is a very important question. A lot of what will dissipate it is being completely open so the energy passes through. I don't lock anywhere. Any block in my body will catch the flow and I'll pick up the whole thing. I continue to express what's going on and then, there is a "process period". This is where I process the whole thing in movement for maybe weeks...months...if the experience is really a shocking one, it may run right up against my issues...then, those issues will be really hot. That's one of the reasons I perform. **The performance absolutely devastates me and rocks my very core.** After I have gone through that experience and having been shaken to my very soul, then there are hours and hours of improvisation where I put back together what has been destroyed in a new way. *I get all the information I need from the experience itself.*

For more info, write:

PAUL OERTEL *c/o The Nancy Spanier Dance Theatre*

P.O. Box 4631 in Boulder, COLORADO 80306

THE RITUAL CATALYST

Master of Ceremonies

by Antero Alli

The ritual catalyst is someone familiar enough with the work itself to suggest appropriate tasks for its challenging integrity and development. This role does not have to function as a director, teacher, guru and/or therapist. S/he can operate quite well as an *overseer* gathering pertinent information for individual and group progress. This includes the knowledge of ongoing **present-time moods, resistances, energy levels** and **the overall spirit** of each meeting for the purpose of introducing ritual designs **amplifying current dynamics.** The catalyst does not have to impose a direction but through careful observation, **reads** the innate tendencies evolving throughout the group as a whole. By serving this amplification process, participants and catalysts alike gain deeper access to the forces at play and where they are going. The effectiveness of ritual ignition seems to depend on this kind of perception.

During the time alloted to ritual preparation, the catalyst has the opportunity to check in on group levels of: Resistance, Committment, Attention Spans and Excitement. These four references offer guidelines to scanning and reading the group mind, as well as individual presence. (Sometimes, it is useful to participate in the Physical Prep especially if it generates greater awareness of the four previous references.) Since the catalyst is, for the most part, experienced by participants as a *VOICE...* there are certain vocal adjustments serving facilitation. It is by verbal suggestion that the catalyst refers participants to various aspects of Self to surrender to. In this way, a rather vulnerable condition is invoked in participants. The catalyst learns to combine words and voice them in ways conducive to ***inviting*** participation, development and eventually, surrender. As a ritual catalyst, we are speaking to participants as Central Nervous Systems and the Bodies they inhabit and manage.

Any individual trained in the medium can function as ritual catalyst and is actually suggested practice for people to take turns doing so. One skill a catalyst learns is **relaxation.** If you're tense, it'll show up in your voice. Resistance excites resistance so it's a good idea to express resistance vocally beforehand and get it out of your system. (Participants have enough of their own resistance to work through without having to sort through yours, too.) The next task is learning how to **observe.** What we are looking for is **present-time dynamics.** A catalyst is there to *register the moment* until enough bits and pieces are gathered to speak about it.

It is quite useless, and even distracting to others, to speak ***before*** observing. Read that last sentence again for a key catalyst's technique. The words you use to issue suggestions and commands may require constant adjustment to coincide with the perpetual influx of changing information. The catalyst needs to be that flexible. When in doubt: **relax then, look to see.**

Another skill useful to ritual catalyzation is an outlook permitting *uncertainty.* Participants diligently prepare towards the ritualization of their Source Relations and from here, their interaction amongst each other. The catalyst is in charge of initiating an atmosphere where this is possible. This, in part, starts with an attitude ...an aura...the catalyst brings to the ritual setting. Along with a non-judmental outlook (letting people be themselves in your presence), the catalyst must posit a heightened focus of **the ritual intent.** In short, the catalyst is responsible for charging the space with a certain mixture of autonomy and discipline. One internal adjustment for setting this in motion is playing with a "lack of self-investment". If the catalyst is too excited or ego-involved, participants will pick up on it and resist his/her suggestions. As the ritual catalyst, create space for the participant's involvement by occasionally removing our own. (Don't make your position Too Important.) ***This does not imply a diminished Self-commitment but a higher degree than previously realized because a catalyst does not require going through the same changes as that which it effects.***

In a highly sensitized Rare Area, *words are mantras* capable of shaping the bodies receiving them. When selecting words and phrases, refrain from those which require the receiver to Think About what you said. **Speak to The Body.** Use simple words and **be clear and direct.** The Body tends to resist over-definition and the imposition of structures onto a basically fluid state. Don't spell things out too much. Experiment with letting instructions be incomplete enough to let participants include their own definitions. (Generally speaking, *the less you say the better.*) You are here to create a space for the discovery process excited by your initial instructions. It is important to give participants ample time to explore and exhaust your suggestions. The Body needs *more time* to experience than The Mind does to get the picture. **Patience** is a catalyst's guide. On the other hand, the pace of a ritual can be quickened by suggesting DEVELOPMENT and/or GESTURES to help detect and frame the emerging material.

The role of the catalyst in the GROUP CIRCLE is simply asking participants to speak about their experience. (This is a good place to pay attention to new information regarding proceeding rituals) If participants start projecting judgments onto themselves/each other or speak too abstractly about their experience, it's the catalyst's responsibility to refer them back to PRESENT TIME... i.e., "What are you feeling **right now** ?" "How did you **relate** to what happened ?" ETC. Here, you are a mirror to the participants... working to help clarify their statements and encouraging them to find **their own words** to describe their process.

The tasks and contact points the catalyst chooses for the group are most effective when they build towards a final, culminating ritual wherein group interplay is the focus. This final ritual should incorporate previous rituals and preps into its scope and create some obvious balance or healing. Due to the attention given to Energy Itself in this medium, rituals tend to excite "psycho-active states" wherein the Central Nervous System is stimulated and occasionally "on fire." Taking this into consideration, the final ritual can be one to help "cool off" participants into unwinding. Besides, the more participants "try" in this work, the more exhausted they become and more prone to resist attending.

One way to support a gentle ending to the ritual session is by turning out all the lights and suggesting participants lay on the floor to assimilate what has occured. This stabilizing factor initiates a "settling phase" often appreciated after the more intensive, charged ceremonies. Any suggestions or instructions restoring **planetary awareness** to participants also works well here. Sometimes, a Group Circle is required to formalize an ending and other times, none is needed at all. Like much of the catalyst's skills, **flexibility to the moment is the rule of thumb**.

In review, **rituals evolve metamorphically.** The catalyst observes this evolution for detecting its innate tendencies and directions. By honoring the intrinsic direction inherent in each ritual, he/she suggests designs for amplifying and eliciting these tendencies further still. At its most effective, ritual catalyzation is a mirror reflecting the patterns of motion perpetually emerging, submerging and growing out of the participant's expression. (See GROUP DYNAMICS IN THE PERFORMANCE MEDIUM: Interview with Keith Berger, for additional information regarding catalyzation)

GROUP DYNAMICS IN THE PERFORMANCE MEDIUM

An Interview with Keith Berger

by Antero Alli

Keith Berger has been a professional Mime Artist in New York City since 1972 after receiving extensive training with The American Mime Theatre under the direction of Paul Curtis, its founder. Since then, he has toured internationally performing his One-Man Shows , as well as writing and performing in BROKEN TOYS, his Mime Musical, which was produced on Off-Broadway in NYC, 1981. Currently, Keith appears in feature films and video productions nationwide. This interview took place in mid-September of 1986 over the telephone while he spoke from his loft studio in New York City.

ANTERO ALLI: *Speak about the role personal freedom plays in relation to your work with group dynamics.*

KEITH BERGER: Personal Freedom... the way in which I try to engender personal freedom from a group is to start off with getting the group in a circle and asking them what their image of themselves is. Then, building on that image and giving them a task of becoming more of that image or agreeing to choose a new image for them... and that's usually in terms of a personal character, a role they play in life... who they see themselves as. Generally, it works out that something new evolves from what they are and not from something that is outside of them. I hold them to the task of saying things and behaving in this new image. It can't be something that they don't agree on or I just lay on them, it's something they agree on with me. It's usually a very exciting proposition to a group of people, individually. It opens an area of freedom for them because they're seeing themselves (they think) as an outside character, which allows them to be able to do certain things they would never allow themselves to do... for example, being more overt with each other or more flirtatious or more thoughtful or taking themselves more seriously. It right away releases the quality of personal freedom.

AA: *How do you excite group morale and when is it necessary ?*

KB: **To excite group morale, you have to know how to have them produce things, little things, that work extremely well.** When they see these things it's almost like a little miracle that they produced, not the director. It's very tricky because you can set it up so well that they'll have a feeling it was, well, the director. If you are very clever in giving them as little as possible to go on and leaving it to them... and they won't like that at first, they don't want you to leave them alone... let's say they put together a scene or little play and you give them ten minutes to do it, quite often what they can get done in that little ten minutes takes hours and hours, and still doesn't look good. Those little things, especially in the beginning, boost group morale. Now there's another thing that starts to set in... they get used to that, and then there's a problem. The thing that hurts group morale is frustration, which often turns to boredom. **Boredom and frustration are actually two very significant states of being for a group.** It's very good when you reach that but a naive group and even professional groups don't realize it. You've got to somehow tell them and have them acknowledge that they are in an area of boredom or frustration. Somehow, let this stew and anticipate conflict because **it'll happen**.

The main thing to drum into them, and this is the only way to get through it, is to tell them that no matter how bored or frustrated they get to consider it as the most challenging and best time to work. Everybody is glad to work when they're inspired... it's easy to come up with ideas and such. I've found that some very deep, significant ideas come out of boredom, frustration and anger. Something's being cooked up... something's stewing and if you keep working... boom! The thing comes out and the tables totally turn around. It's a bit of a rollercoaster ride. The main thing is to work through it. ***If you keep on trying to inspire a group, you're making a mistake because you're depending on inspiration alone and the group becomes too dependent on the catalyst, or director... their brains kind of turn to mush, like Kindergarten Time.*** So. that period of low morale is generally significant of boredom or frustration. The only thing to do, in my eyes, is to hold the group to working through it and make sure that people have an understanding **before** this occurs.

AA: What are the rules you set down, if any, for the purpose of working towards a product ?

KB: **First of all, the very beginning of the whole process is very important. The product should start to be realized in the very beginning even as a vague image or as a general dynamic or quality of what the show will look like.** They may not get an image of what exactly it is. If they do, in fact, get an image of exactly it is it may not be so good, as that makes it a little too finite. It's important to impress upon a group that no matter how good you think this can be, it's going to turn out to be something else. And that what it turns out to be is better than anything you can imagine. Another rule, or procedure, is having them all keep a log and put certain entities into it...

like observations of people they see... thoughts... memories amd another page for dreams they have during the night... another page for personal goals. It should be like a lifebook. They should limit it to doing it only 10 minutes a day.

Another rule on this time thing. Rehersals should be confined to the shortest time possible. In fact, one thing I've found is in giving them not enough time so it's so concentrated and they have to use their minds. Another rule is to not betray anyone to anybody outside of the group. Keep everything in-house. Try and keep the gossip between you. Another rule is establishing a precedent of competition... ***friendly competition.*** There's always going to be conflict in a good group. Everyone should somehow agree that this is to be an ensemble... that the company would be an All Star no-star company and think that way. I try not to think in terms of rules.

AA: What do you personally try and stay away from in order to remain true to your vision ?

KB: What I try and stay away from is pushing too much of my own prejudices on a group. I have to find out what they're about. I have to help them actualize a... group animal, and a "look" that's theirs. If I impose a look on them, they start depending on me and that's **not** where the best product is gotten.

AA: How is the best product gotten ?

KB: **The best product is gotten if I can take them past where they're used to going and have them look at it.** I'm their third eye. I can see when they start to get a look. Or when they go past what's usual for them. This somehow makes it become real and tangible. If I say everybody do this and look like this, it's not as good. The best things are gotten when somebody has a concept and we all work together to create that concept but it'll be a whole new thing... it won't look the way I first saw it or whoever had the concept.

AA: How would you describe "the miraculous" and the components necessary for its expression ?

KB: First of all, you need (and I hate to say this) talented individuals. Even if they're naive, they have to come from at least a creative thinking orientation. They have to be willing to work real hard and keep working. Taking this talented group, you have to start showing them miracles real soon. **Something's miraculous when it goes beyond their vision yet it is part**

of the image they're growing on or into. It takes honing. This miraculous thing is often raw and it takes writing skills to make it complete and satisfying. One has to bring out in them things they've never seen before or they've had an inkling of. It takes a great amount of personal and group freedom to create this. A lot of it has to do with their own surprise at what they can do. If you can get them into that state, they don't know that they can't be miraculous.. The biggest key, I think, is to convince them that they can, dissolving all beliefs that they can't. One thing about a professional performer is that while they've got obvious skills, they're not so quick to think they can be much greater than what they're capable of projecting.

AA: How can you tell when someone has real talent ?

KB: It takes a certain willingness to be open. A lot of it is in the eyes and quite often very introverted or shy people can be... you have to go by your instincts. The best test is to really take a look at them and inside them, and this is an experience thing. You start to develop a kind of intuition about a person and whether they're going to ring... there's a certain sparkle that comes through... a potential... and this is the job of a catalyst. I think a good catalyst, or director, can recognize these signals. What to look for exactly is very hard for me to put a finger on. *It's instinct, really.*

For more info, write:
THE KEITH BERGER MIME STUDIO
579 Broadway --Third Floor, New York City, NY 10012

DANGERS?!

Perils & Pitfalls Along the Way

Unscrupulous ritual occurs during any diminshment of individual and/or collective integrity, wherein some form of invasion or violation takes place. There's nothing wrong or bad about this per se, unless it continues to persist. Violation of integrity is simply a sign of being off the track and is a mistake. **Everybody makes mistakes.** The ritual functions serve to protect the integrity of this medium and require diligent practice to maintain. These guidelines have been developed to create a safe place to play in a High Risk Zone, where the volatile conditions of experiencing the Unknown are tempered and contained. There are several *known* dangers recorded from the ritual theatre archives and all relate to potential perils and pitfalls of Source Relations. These dangers can be related to other systems which explore Archetypal contact, psychology and practice, as well.

IRRITATION

One of the effects of exposure to intensity and energetic acceleration is over-stimulation. In its excess, there develops an overall sense of irritation which turns into numbness if it's not caught in time. In its extreme, there is a kind of "short-circuit" from Information Overdose. All in all, the Info O.D. and the psychic constipation it causes result from neglecting to permit assimilation time for digesting the new experiences often absorbed in ritual work. New information can be very exciting. **If one fails to recognize when one has Had Enough, stimulation starts its conversion to irritation.** Irritation can also occur with "forced catharsis". This occurs in those moments where we try and push expression or emotional release faster than its natural pace. Irritation happens when we are overwhelmed by the charged contents of our own subconscious/unconscious. One result is the over-amping of the intellectual/interpretive circuitry, thus leaving one helpless to describe and integrate the experience. Sometimes, in dramatic examples, the motivation to communicate withers and eventually loses its purpose altogether.

DISSIPATING IRRITATION

1) The function of the PHYSICAL WARM-UP is **fortification**. FEELING THE BODY DEEPLY generates the essential substance to fortify our integrity. This substance, or density, helps absorb the shocks of Source Relations. This fortification works like insulation around an electrical

cable...the thicker the cable, the more juice you can run through it without the danger of short-circuiting. A good WARM-UP insulates the cable.

2) NO-FORM **neutralizes** charge (or that element responsible for excitement and resistance). After an especially charged contact point and/or ritual, it is suggested practice to enter a deeper and longer NO-FORM to dissipate its hold on you. The greater the charge (positive or negative), the greater the NO-FORM required for restoring balance.

3) When irritation results from **too much clarity**, it is suggested practice to explore rituals to access **density as a value.** If density is resisted (as being "wrong" or from fear of losing clarity), construct the ritual to include accessiing **resistance to density**. Polarities which can facilitate this conversion: TOP/BOTTOM, EARTH/AIR, DENSITY/CLARITY,
1stCHAKRA/7thCHAKRA, SATURN/JUPITER, BODY/SPIRIT,
SEEING/FEELING.

4) To heal the mind from intellectual blow-out, design a mandala with different colored pens and paper to symbolize the experience through color, shape and design. Another device is in extracting a myth from the experience and writing a story describing and evoking it again.

5) Irritation/short-circuit develops with a holding pattern of becoming **attached to the intensity** of the experience. Often times, attachment to the energy/power occurs when we don't believe/feel that we are ENOUGH the way we are already. We resist letting go because we are ignorant of our true self...that, we are a piece of god and god is enough. God is. The alternative to this kind of attachment can be found for oneself through meditation, silent prayer and long walks in nature. **Practice NO-FORM.**

6) The ritual function of **sanctification** develops the awareness of space as a value, thus is helpful in dissipating irritation. It does so by minimizing obsessive tendencies often times associated with not knowing when to stop. Design rituals to deepen sanctification.

SHADOW-BOXING

As we encounter aspects of our Self, it is natural to begin including these into a more "wholesome" Self-image than before. Sometimes, during the preliminary phase of Self-identification (INITIATIONS), the ego or self-image crystallizes on one aspect over another at the cost of repressing its opposite, "alter-ego". In time, the alter-ego develops in the subconscious as a Shadow figure taking archetypal forms of...The Devil, Death, The Boogeyman and so forth. *If* this Shadow side is not evoked consciously and included into the Self-image, then it is unconsciously projected onto living persons most resembling the personification of ones inner Shadow, ***whatever that may be***. The Shadow is a threat to the aspect of oneself most closely identified with because once it surfaces, it cancels out that cherished aspect via polarizations and ego-death. If we remain ego-attached during the encounter with Shadow, then when our ego crumbles we may believe we are ACTUALLY DYING. The panic and desperation arriving with this delusion is potentially very dangerous, especially if big decisions are made during the collapsing process.

Ego naturally trembles in the wake of a greater truth than itself. Ego-death is a response to outdated Self-concepts dissolving from the impact of Self. It is often Pride and Vanity that choose to identify with one aspect over another, especially if they fall in love with one which glorifies and aggrandizes the ego itself. Such an ego becomes the inevitable subject for ritual sacrifice when we learn how to *UNBOX THE SHADOW.*

UNBOXING THE SHADOW

1) Design a ritual for encountering the Shadow. (See DARK RITES of the Soul in the Ritual Design Section). Dialogue with it until you feel ready to personify it to embrace and become the Shadow aspect.

2) Design a ritual for locating the aspect you are stuck on, then name its opposite. Set up a polarization ritual and locate your point of balance. Alternate between both sides until you don't have to be either one. This will help neutralize their collective charge.

re: PSYCHIC GARBAGE

In the more cathartic phases of the work, we are often subject to not only our own emotional discharge but that of others. As we move through the multiple layers of our conditioned responses, psychic exfoliation is inevitable and there comes a time when people have to learn how to own their shit, or at least understand how to process it without imposing it on others. This area of Taking Out the Psychic Garbage is highly personal in that everybody has, more or less, differing tolerance levels for toxic psychic absorbtion. The more refined our sensitivities become, the more acute our impressions of psychic dirt. The first thing to be aware of is the smell of our own shit. Detecting the distinction between our garbage and that of anothers is preliminary to Taking Out Our Own...and letting others Take Out Theirs. This can be initiated after each ritual by calling back and **reclaiming the projections** used to charge the setting in the first place.

Electrically speaking, auras collect static in those areas prone to intense concentration, condensation and/or obsession. When one energy center or body area is over-emphasized, excess energetic residue results in that particular region. Another way psychic garbage is taken out is by mobilizing your energy field. Don't over-emphasize one center over others. If, for example, the Head Center is too psycho-active...put yourself through Emotional Changes. If you're too emotionally involved, try abstracting yourself Into Your Head for awhile. Putting yourself through changes will generally mobilize auric forces sufficiently to minimize accumulation of electrical static in any one area of your field. If static does collect, let your hands act like magnets and have them scan for static for the purpose of sucking it up into your palms. Then, flick off the static. Taking showers can also cleanse away not only excess static, but other people's energy, as well.

Electrical static can collect in the corners of a room. One ritual school confesses to several sharp and loud handclaps in these corners to break up the garbage. (This same school insisted it had to be two **or** four claps, for some reason unknown to this author, yet it does carry the effect of "owning the corners" if not anything else.) Incense like sage, cedar or frankincence are good for breaking up stinky energies. Opening up windows and doors, while directing the energies out as if you were sweeping the room also seems to brighten the space.

The planetary entity seems to process negative energy quite well, as do its canine and feline ambassadors...dogs and cats. Once again, any relationsyhip with the living entity of Earth will excite all kinds of hereto unknown services. Energy expelled from ourselves during ritual is still at our command and it is up to us to command it to a place wherein it will transform. Commanding energy down to the core of the planet for processing is another way to maintain planetary relations while cleansing your aura and the space around you. If you are too concerned with polluting the planet, construct a sphere of neutral energy above your head and let it magnetize all of your expended energy to itself...then, connect this sphere down to your solar plexus with a beam. Program the sphere to start sending down the energy it has neutralized. Direct this neutral energy into your solar plexus where it may re-distribute it throughout your entire system again.

Another way of cleaning a ritual space energetically is through high-energy chanting (see the Homing Sonic Meditation in VOCAL CREATIONS). Sonic resonance will work best when it is focused on accelerating the overall energy in the room, i.e., resonating from the Heart Center on up. It helps to also know what your ritual intent is...why are you doing this? With a strong intent, it's easier to know what kinds of energies you're after and which ones you're looking to bypass. Without an intent, you run the risks that come with the territory of a psychic sewer system. After executing particularly charged rituals, some effort ought to be made towards Taking Out the Garbage. Due to the highly personal nature of Everybody's Shit, we are all individually responsible for cleaning up our mess.

EGO-INFLATION

When relating to and identifying with Archetypal forces, the personal self is known to change shape by shrinking and/or puffing up, refered to hereafter as negative and positive ego-inflation, respectively. Inflation is inevitable with sudden and thorough influxes of new information and energy. In positive inflation, the ego identifies itself with BEING THE SOURCE and puffs up with self-importance. With negative inflation, ego negates itself through distorted comparison with Source and feels unworthy and defeated. Both forms of inflation are necessary for first-hand knowledge of recognizing ones own ego-tendencies. *The ego puffs up by merging with something more powerful than its secretly helpless self in order to create the illusion of its omnipotence by*

association. Ego will shrink when it feels like it must prostrate itself to an omnipotent source that is constantly out of its reach and communion. Both types of inflation reflect ways we have been looking at ourselves. **Their dangers are two-fold:**

1) Both keep us out of PRESENT-TIME by our preoccupation with feeling significant and/or diminished **by a previous experience;**

2) Both cultivate self-doubt, fear and eventually paranoia when we discover the World does not conform to our distorted self-image.

On the whole, ego-inflation is a necessary phase in our capacity to identify, become and TO BE. The delusion sets in when we confuse our ego (Self-image) with who we are (Self)and start taking ourselves too seriously. **It is quite possible that we are not required to be anything at all.**

DEFLATIONARY TACTICS

1) **Inflation becomes an issue when we resist NO-FORM.** Give yourself permission to be nothing without it being meaningful or meaningless, but a **neutral refuge** from concept, expression and/or form. Who are you ?

2) **If you are attached to The Meaningful,** incorporate The Meaningless through a polarization ritual until you get them both out of your system. If you are "puffed up", **make a fool of youself.** Explore CHAOS. Laugh at yourself, then laugh at yourself laughing at yourself.

3) **When the self is too full of itself,** it needs to empty. You can take charge of this before Universe takes over by the device of **alienation**. Be alone for awhile. Enforce a day or two of complete isolation without any human contact, if possible. If you cannot get away from others, go on a Talk Fast..**be silent and surrender to the solitude it yields.**

4) Occasionally, inflation expresses itself as the overwhelming feeling one is part of something Cosmically Profound and...one is! However, simultaneously, one is in the midst of Unbearable Absurdity, as well. Additional polarities to be explored include: SINCERE/PHONY; TRUTH/LIES; SIGNIFICANT/POINTLESS; COSMIC/MUNDANE; COMEDY/TRAGEDY.

5) **The value of NO-FORM can not be over-estimated** for disengaging ones identification from one form or another of Self. For the purpose of the ritual itself, it is useful to BE something but it is limiting to believe one is simply that one aspect of the Multidimensional Self. There exists a conversion from BEING A FORCE **to** PLAYING THE FORCE which emerges with practice. PLAYING A FORCE requires no identification whatsoever yet recalls the experience for reference. In PLAYING, the force moves through you without getting stuck on you or versa visa. It is in this way that the phase of identification **forms the basis for advanced work.** One way of telling there is a true development is in the capacity for PLAY. A light-hearted approach lends mobility and grace to any ritual. Our being is renewed in NO-FORM. It protects us by cultivating detachment. NO-FORM is neutral ground permitting return to deeper living by virtue of its perspective. NO-FORM is regenerating. When we are being nothing, we are simply being ourselves.

6) Sit with a partner and maintain eye contact. One asks the other: "WHO ARE YOU?" as the other responds. With each response, the asker repeats the question in a variety of intonations, always **doubting** the answers given by the other. Follow through until an end is appropriate and/or until you get it. Then, reverse roles and repeat. The intent here is direct-knowledge of our tendencies to think we know who we are thus, falling into the hypnotic spell resultant from being convinced that we can refer to our mysterious core by any name, image or concept at all!

7) **When the self-image has become distorted** enough to affect coordination and physical balance, the ego must find ways to become **the same size as the physical body to regain its footing.** One sure way of coordinating these two aspects is by putting yourself to work at hard, physical labor, i.e., digging ditches, gardening, moving heavy objects, etc. It is best if your work benefits another or a group. Service and gratitude are wonderous antidotes to excess inflation.

8) **For negative inflation,** attempt the task of suspending judgment and comparison. These intellectual functions can be replaced by your ability to PAY ATTENTION and SILENTLY WITNESS the wonder of unity. Gradually and gently begin including yourself as a piece of that unity and not as someone who "thinks" they are outside of it. Set up a polarity: ISOLATION/UNITY; 3rd Chakra/5th Chakra; EQUALITY/HEIRARCHY; WILL/COMMUNICATION.

GRACE AS AN IMPEDIMENT

Ironically enough, grace is an impediment to some. Grace gets in the way when our techniques become so refined and slick that we create the illusion of our spontaneity ***and believe it.*** This is the delusion sophistication casts not only with oneself but those naive enough to fall sway to the spell. (Nothing can be more enchanting than being in the presence of someone who is thoroughly under the influence of his/her own enchantment coupled with the subtlety and grace of charm.) The mechanics of charisma are known to but a few and among these, a choice must be made or it will be made for us. This decision entails a social responsibility involving the personal advancement of others. ***We only trip over our grace when we have too much of it.*** Once we find the internal/external adjustments for circulating our grace among others and catalyzing it in them, we are liberated as **liberators of others**. If we forgo this social responsibility,the Greater Grace of Universal Intelligence will generate power plays, corruptions and a variety of scandals to guarantee our inevitable fall. Once we reach a stable degree of self-empowerment, our next step is empowering others...

CIRCULATING GRACE

1) **Accept your power** and wear your charisma like a necklace instead of a ball and chain. Redefine "power" by your capacity to empower others and excite advancement in their lives. *Circulate the riches.*

2) **Render pleasure contagious.** Be a source of uplifting inspiration for those around you. Recognize the creative, progressive side to every sad story you hear and refuse to buy into people's Martyr Complexes.

3) **Annihilate heirarchy** whenever it starts up in relation to you, especially with those confused individuals who insist on setting you up on a pedestal and/or wanting discipleship. A disciple is an Asshole looking for somebody to attach itself to. To assume is to make an "ass" out of "u" and "me."

4) With every advancement in your personal/economic/spiritual evolution, bring somebody else up in the same spirit you are being uplifted. **Link up.**

5) Explore those rituals dedicated to ILLUMINATIONS, as they can provide an outlet for grace... especially for those which are alchemical in nature and are structured to parallel development in the Plant Kingdom.

6) **If you are already falling from grace** and wish to quicken the descent, explore the rituals integrating the biblical polarities of ANGELS & DEMONS (see DARK RITES of the SOUL)... as in ANGELS IN HELL and DEMONS IN HEAVEN.

These have been the primary dangers recorded throughout a decade of ritual practice and hopefully, some relevant antidotes to chase the poisons down and out. ***In review, all dangers seem to result from diminishment of individual and/or group integrity, wherein some form of violation occurs.*** Most times these are unintentional and quite unexpected, yet they arise from the fragility of the human instrument struggling to serve its Maker. Throughout this struggle, mistakes are made and then hopefully rectified through adjustment. Without making mistakes, however, we can be sure there are not enough risks being taken into regions unknown. It takes courage to make mistakes and absolute genius to confess them. This is because mistakes are "God Leaks" and point the way, often times, to places we'd never even think about going.

CHAPEL PERILOUS

Occasionally, there occurs a stage of personal disorientation so profound as to approach the perilous. Chapel Perilous is a name given to that place where souls go when they leave their bodies... also known as the Dark Night of the Soul. (Read *ANGEL TECH,* Chapel Perilous section; Falcon Press) I've seen this occur in myself and others after prolonged and effective polarization work wherein the union of opposites becomes almost unbearable to the rational mind. Unless the intellect is trained to permit ambiguity, uncertainty, and confusion, it may tend to "short-circuit" while attempting to figure out the interplay of contraries occuring within oneself. This innate confusion threatens the intellect's self-defining capacity for comprehension. Certain phases of internal development are best left alone and not meddled with intellectually and, ***this is one of them.***

One way I've minimized intellectual panic during epic disorientation is by studying the alchemical maps of Carl C. Jung as outlined in his book, *The Psychology of theTransference..* During those moments where ego and Self merge, there is released **a good amount of light**. Like the photons released from proton/electron fusions, this illumination does not last and **the brighter the flash, the darker the afterward.** Alchemically speaking, the marriage of opposites preceeds the funeral of the "death" phase. The greater the union, the greater the death and eventually, the rebirth. From an alchemical perspective, ***the "blacker the death"... the "whiter the cleansing" phase proceeding it.*** In this light, death is refered to as the start of the "great work" and everything preceeding it, the preparation. It is in this "black earth" death phase that most of the work goes underground (into the Subconscious) to gestate. As seeds germanate only in the dark, we are asked to hang out in "a dark place" until the sprouts of a new soul begin emerging from our depths. (See ALCHEMY section in *ANGEL TECH).*

A new level of soul-consciousness is born whenever our vision has integrated polarity into its perspective. ***Soul*** is a word to describe the degree by which we reflect the wholeness of Spirit, God and/or Source. Soul develops with the inclusion of more aspects of our being and I've seen this happen through effective polarization work. While the fusion of opposites goes underground to cook, the conceptual mind is left alone to make sense of things. The abyss left over is what it feels like to be inside Chapel Perilous. Emotions of abandonment are common, as are those of *drowning and terror*. The value of perseverance and self-committment are paramount during these times where **Faith** is worth its weight in gold. From an intellectual perspective, **there are no guarantees here.** The future may feel non-existant and produce feelings of anxiety in a body accustomed to following directions and knowing where to go. If the intellect is unwilling to surrender its habit of Figuring Things Out, it may revert to a tyrant and attempt to control us with paranoid fantasies, delusions of grandeur and other rationalizations for avoiding the encounter with its limited understanding. The alternative to conceptual convulsions is the humbling process of confessing ignorance and learning an attitude of intellectual service as a **translator** rather than a "creator".

Perhaps the most useful device I've uncovered during these Dark Nights is ***disidentification.*** Fears may run willy-nilly and delusions hurly-burly, yet we are **not** obliged to become any of it. Herein, **NO-FORM** provides sanctum and refuge. To the degree we are easy with not having to be anybody or anything, is the degree we can create the inner space essential for the emerging soul to return and re-integrate itself. Without this space, Dark Nights have been known to take more time. A way the intellect can serve (instead of inflict fearful control) is in distinguishing itself from the happenings, imagined and otherwise. It can do this by working to articulate what it sees in a manner most precise, poetic and/or artistic. Once our identity is extracted from the countless impressions and images we have of ourselves, it is possible to become more receptive to something higher, or true. (See *ANGEL TECH*: 7th Grade, ALCHEMY)

Polarizations work to neutralize charge. Sometimes, the Dark Night characterizes itself by an all-time low energy level. This may express itself as depression, apathy, lethargy and other signposts of Hitting Bottom. This often results from having been previously identified with the charge of the polarity being polarized. Once the charge is neutralized and released,the ego wobbles aimlessly searching for a new definition. This is where it can get dangerous. As a response to trauma, ego automatically fixes itself to something or someone to temporarily stabilize itself, thus initiating the start of a potential obsssion. The object of obsession is not the cause but is often selected randomly as the nearest, easiest promise of security.

One antidote to obsession is humor; *if* something is really true, then it's also probably very funny. Another obsession-disperser is going the other way and dramatizing the Dark Night through conducting your very own funeral. This kind of "living funeral" can be done alone, with a Significant Other and/or an entire group willing to partake in the ceremony. As with any ritual, preparation is everything. Gather all the incruements like incense, candles, music, and whatever else you need to set up a space not only to die in but to be dead in. If you like, write an epitaph or a liturgy articulating the current state of your personal darkness. I have executed these alone, with another and in groups with much success.

Sometimes, when somebody stumbles into the Chapel and fails to realize where they are, it is suggested to seek professional help. One side-effect of "being-out-of-the-body" is Accident Prone behavior which, as we know, can be hazardous to our health. If you know anyone who is tripping over things and hurting themselves unconsciously at an increasing rate, do what you can to help. Jungian psychotherapists (if they've done their homework) will know all about the Dark Night of the Soul and its various treatment procedures. (If they don't, keep searching for those that do. Dark Nights are not easily diagnosed by traditional methods unaccustomed to the process of psychic death and rebirth.) Often times, professional help can be bypassed with ***the right information and several good friends...*** those who can let us go through our changes and not judge us for leaving one "personality shell" behind for something more innate to ourselves. These friends are the acting priests inside Chapel Perilous. A little bit of love goes a long, long way and never underestimate the power of a few kind words.

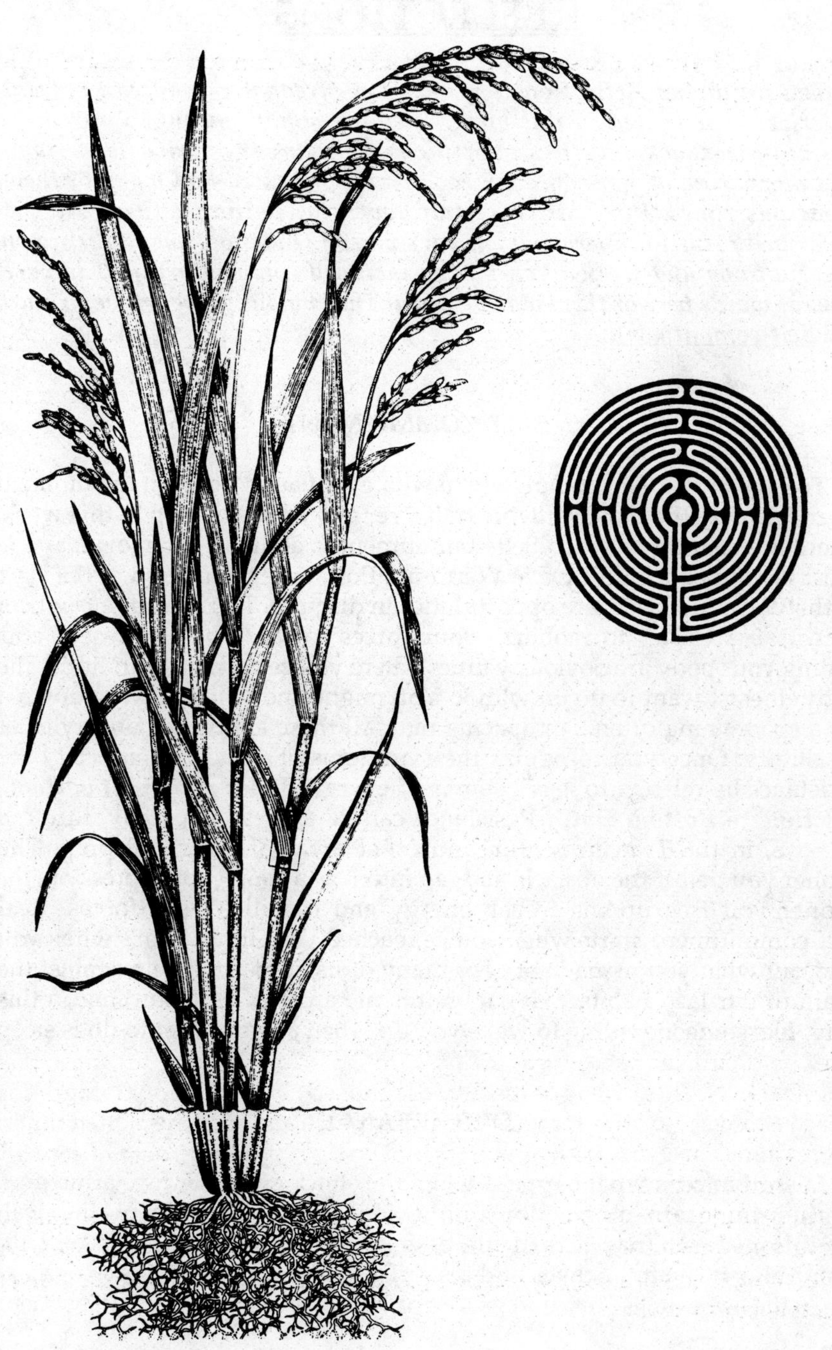

REFLECTIONS

The following Reflections are my own personal responses to ritual practice as presented in this book. They are simply meant to provide a source of feedback ...a series of opinions regarding the various aspects of this work. Having gone through each ritual presented and many of them numerous times, I've noticed certain repeating patterns. These are not necessarily true for Everybody, as each person tends to come to their own observations and truths. Yet, I have included commentary just in case several words here or there may be useful.The obvious place for me to start is ...Self-commitment.

SELF-COMMITMENT

To give of yourself completely to whatever you're doing at the moment is undeniably the most valuable trait I've learned to develop in this work. There are also times when Self-commitment is at an all-time low... and is most obvious during Physical Warm-up. Bottoms encountered at the start of the Warm-up cycle are opportunities in disguise. Those moments where it feels *impossible* to mobilize your forces towards being present and feeling your body are obviously times where you've reached your limit. The body doesn't want to go on with it. You might find yourself lying down a lot... or yawning often... or spacing out. All these and more, are styles of resistance. Once you recognize the symptoms, it's easier to **sanctify** the resistance by relating to it as **a source of energy.** ***When you've hit bottom, it's time to Bottom Out.*** Resistance can be expressed vocally, through gesture, in the Transitory Run and other areas of the ritual prep. The sooner you detect the obstacle and tap into it as a source for expression, the sooner you free up the frozen energy and mobilize your forces. Real Self-committment **starts** when you've reached your limit. That's when you find out what you're made of. For many of us, it means going against the grain of our lazy habits. Self-committment can even be disturbing in this way, like someone trying to wake you up when all you want to do is sleep late.

DISTURBANCE

Disturbance is what happens when the shock of new information goes against-the-grain of previous indoctrination. When the mechanical, conditioned self has a difficult time of digesting a truth, it will do everything it can to upchuck and resist. Disturbance supports development when the agitation is **used to wake up**. Such an internal adjustment requires: 1) **Hard work** and 2) **A willingness to wake up**. Growth is rarely comfortable unless, of course, one is learning comfort in order to grow. In short, birth hurts...always has.

There is a conflict arising, from the friction of disturbance, which generates an essential **substance** for growth. Substance can be accumulated by understanding progressive disturbance...**how to put the conflict to work.** This conflict is symbolic of internal rebellion whereby one aspect of ourselves is attempting to overthrow another. This is the unresolved substance drama is made of. Conflict, by itself, does not negate harmony; quite the contrary. True harmony exists only in relation to true discord, as only a true form emerges from chaos. Chaos, in this way, remains our inevitable origin of structure, direction and eventually, clarity.

CREATIVE CONDITIONS

As creation expresses itself differently through each individual, so do the ideal conditions for exciting the creative process. Each person must find their own way of catalyzing a creative state. One individual's way of setting it up may be in direct conflict with another's. We are all responsible for creating that Rare Area by which the creative thrives best in, lest our minds begin reading our creative process as a Disaster Area. One question we might ask is: ***"What is a creative state ?" or "What requires completing before I can trigger a creative state?".*** There are certain attitudes and "blocks" which impede the setting up of a Rare Area. Unless these blocks are recognized and eliminated, our creative energy will tend to turn in on itself and implode. ***It seems that idiosyncratic activity, movement and expression are intimately connected with igniting and maintaining a creative state.*** (We create when we're alone in ourselves, ie., at one with ourself.) This starts by finding out what is most highly personal to oneself then, linking with these objects, symbols and activities for generating personal power. It's true that too many cooks spoil the broth.

OBSTACLE ORIENTATION

One of the more frustrating responses to resistance is resisting it. If we're too involved with attacking what's eating at us, we usually lose sight of what we were fighting for in the first place. There's a way to deal with resistance that's kind of like detective work. You learn to know ***its smell, its track, its tension...***you figure resistance out. Once you're able to detect it, your mobility increases tenfold. **Obstacle Orientation is a progressive style of entering a High Resistance Zone.** You enter looking for the tiger...knowing you're a lot better off **seeing it** amidst the jungle tangle than **not knowing** where it is at all. This takes a subtle kind of skill lest it becomes another way of resisting. When a real hunter stalks a wild beast, s/he prays to that creature, regarding it as sacred. This is the meaning behind the **sanctification of resistance.** ***You set up communication lines with the enemy by seeking out your secret affinity first.***

THE INTERNAL CONTRACT

How commmited and devoted are you to being alive and happy on this planet? Everyone alive is married and only death itself grants divorce. This marriage is between none other than body and spirit, whose interpenetration gives birth to the soul. The body, with its needs, fears and wisdom is primarily devotional by nature in that it passively obeys whatever orders it receives. The spirit has its intent to manifest. Without a body, it has no way of materializing its intent. To the degree spirit and body lack crucial information about the other, is the degree they are in conflict. **The soul develops from intersecting points between body and spirit expressive of mutual affinity.** The heart opens only after spirit and body get along with each other. These are principles from which it has been easy to comprehend the Internal Contract between spirit and body for the development of a soul.

The soul is the means by which experience is possible at all. The biological instrument of the soul is the Central Nervous System...the intermediary between spirit and body...physiologically, between DNA and the muscle fibers required to execute genetic instructions. **All we ever need to know is within our body.** The cells, neurons and DNA contain vast storehouses of ancestral and past-life memory, present-time survival information and the direction of future evolution. The soul's journey ignites into experience everything we are capable of knowing. Before the soul can travel, however, certain contracts have to be drawn up and signed.

Self-commitment is an internal contract between Spirit and Body, negotiated by Soul. Soul doesn't evolve until spirit and body come to some kind of understanding. For example: The Body's needs, essential strengths and frailities must be recognized, heard and spoken to...otherwise The Body resists. The Body is more willing to undergo immense changes when included in the Big Picture. So, it behooves us to **speak to the body**. It benefits all concerned to know its needs, desires and fears as well as its rewards. The animal requires rewards to sustain the gratification necessary for being motivated to live on this planet. What are yours? Once discovered, don't promise youself them unless you KEEP YOUR WORD. It's counter-productive to break promises with yourself and The Body takes time to build back the trust after this kind of betrayal.

Spirit relates to The Body as a vehicle to manifest its intent. If the spirit doesn't understand The Body, it may try and force its intent. As souls, we tend to experience spiritual intent through purpose. The body's central purpose is in BEING FELT. Spirit's purpose is in BEING SEEN. When The Body is felt, it's more malleable and receptive to spirit's intent... just as when spirit is SEEN, it becomes more sensitive to The Body's need to be felt. This is one basis for stabilizing the internal contract enabling the spirit to be materialized and the body to spiritualize. When we are FELT AND SEEN, it's easier to be LOVED and thus, realize the Soul's purpose. We may need to be affirmed as animals (FELT) and spirits (SEEN) before Soul consciousness awakens within ourselves. It takes a strong ego, or self-concept, to embrace our contraries...the Human Being we are. To simultaneously honor animal and spirit needs, a tremendous compassion and tolerance is called for. This is impossible if we are in judgment of either side. When both sides of our mysterious nature are allowed to exist together, ***a miracle is born.***

THE WARM UP

Preparation is everything. An effective warm-up is essential for effective ritual. One question I like to ask is, "What are we warming up to?" or "What are we preparing for?" and, of course, "Why are we here?". The contemplation of these questions can sanctify an entire warm-up cycle. In some way, we are warming up to God...to the Unknown...to offer ourselves to the Source. The sanctification process is especially important as that's how the ritual begins. The motions, sounds, and gestures used to express blessings and safety to the space also need to accomodate the awareness of others in the room. Sanctification calls upon us to **permit being, ours and that of others.** ***If the spirit of sanctification is strong enough, it can be infused right into the meditation phase of the warm-up, turning this stage into prayer itself.*** The spinal, stretching and sweating phases which follow can then emerge from a sacred origin. Sweat, in this light, is Holy water. Sometimes the warm-up doesn't go so well. People are wrapped up in their frustrations, resistances and inertias. When this happens, it is an urgent signal to detect the blocks and then begin sanctifying the resistance by giving it expression through sound, tension, motion and anything to release its grip on us. It is a critical point, really. **The time of greatest resistance-boredom-frustration is the best time to express the depth of your commitment...*which does wonders for morale.***

NO-FORM

NO-FORM is the *crux* of ritual. To the degree ***intimacy with void*** becomes a value is the extent that the rituals themselves carry life, form and substance. NO-FORM is responsible for true transformation. It enables us to move between different forms of expression elicited by the various contact points. The word "transform" literally means to move between one form to another. NO-FORM is the bridge making this possible. Even though NO-FORM is important, it is also ***nothing special.*** Those who have mistakenly identified NO-FORM as The Absolute Truth tend to homogenize their personalities by turning Bland and Faceless. The antidote to this is none other than exploring **Life After Zen,** or seeing the relative nature of All Things and NO-FORM is **one of All Things.** It does not have to be a goal or destination to be effective. ***In the big picture, NO-FORM is a multi-purpose tool for transformation.*** One more thing. It is *useless* to think about NO-FORM. Whatever you think it is, it isn't. Even the word "NO-FORM" is **not it** but a way to refer to the experience.

NO-FORM teaches *dissolution.* It helps us dissove our attachment to any given form of expression. This supports the creative process by minimizing stagnation...the Staying In One Place Too Long syndrome. **Any expression fully lived can be left behind while passing through the transition of its decay. Attachment to anything undergoing decay is pain.** In this way, NO-FORM is a refuge during times of great transition. Our relationship to our true nature via NO-FORM deepens with each layer of the journey to our center. No matter what we think we are, NO-FORM reminds us that we are not that. NO-FORM disperses our tendency to identify with the various activities we mistake for our true identity: our body, emotions, thoughts, opinions, bias, behavior, etc. Through its experience, we are able to gradually accumulate perspective. **Through its absence, we lose touch with our Source and forget that it is not I, you, or it that we are here for. No-FORM is a Spiritual Emergency Break.**

NAUSEA

On occasion, individuals have complained of a physical and/or emotional nausea from doing the work. This has come up often as a response to NO-FORM by those individuals with little or no previous experience with relating to Void. My understanding is that the area of the solar plexus undergoes a mild to dramatic **shock** resulting in this kind of nausea. (The solar plexus is that network of nerves in direct contact with the intestinal tract, as well as being the power center of the ego itself...the personal will.) Since prerequisites for NO-FORM include **relaxing the desire to control,** personal relationship with Void is often disconcerting to the uninitiated. Once the will has been trained in the discipline of releasing control (to expand its power), then intestinal resistance dissipates as we are ready to "stomach" the experience of Nothingness. To assimilate the shock of No-Form, I suggest becoming more responsible for your safety...so, you can **afford** to be more vulnerable. Thus, emphasize the Rare Area, Little Circle and Sanctification in general.

TALKING ABOUT IT

Talking is a *dispersion device.* It releases steam...hot air. Sometimes it's useful to disperse pressure and other times, absolutely fatal. When one has had significant emotional and psychic input, there is a tendency to want to tell others...***to "share."*** Sometimes, when a certain experience has not been completely digested and understood **for oneself yet,** one trips over words trying to describe what happened. This is a sign that you are not yet ready to talk about it. You may want to write about it or draw pictures or play music. Another aspect of Talking About It is the element of **secrecy**. If one is onto something **truly of value to oneself**, perhaps it is best not to spill ones death too soon ? Talking disperses power. At times, it's necessary to vent excess energy and other times, restraint is required to stop us from pissing our lives away...

ON "DYING"

Initiation rituals have a lot to do with to do with what I'll call *dying.* Dying occurs when the collapse of our pretentions and preconceptions reveals who we actually are. ***Dying is the sacred task of Dropping Ones Act towards surrendering to a deeper part of ourselves than the personality...the persona or "act."*** It's most difficult to comprehend after becoming persona-identified and believing we are actually and literally dying. **Dying helps us disengage from our act.** ***Dying is that empty time where nothing happens.*** Our willingness to commit to this Dead Zone is often a good way to realize the process of psychic death/rebirth. At the darkest, stillest moment there's a big excitement that occurs...like a blue spark hitting your brain. There are absolutely no guarantees whatsoever and everytime it's a different outcome yet, there's a certainty that can be counted on with dying and that's... **rebirth.** When nothing is happening on the surface, you can be sure that a hell of a lot is going on down under. It only takes time, commitment and perseverence to see it through for yourself. Dying is like anything else, in a way. You just cook it until it pops out of the oven.

SELF-CONSCIOUSNESS

It is natural to feel awkward around others in an asocial setting. We all get "self-conscious" while wondering if anybody is watching us. We all spy on others to see how they're doing. Sometimes, it's necessary to go through this and get it out of your system. One adjustment which seems to diminish this kind of self-consciousness is the reminder that each person is there to work **for themselves** and to deepen the Self-commitment necessary for Source Relations. If it helps, ***make a fool of yourself and get it over with*****....the fool that persists in his/her folly becomes wise...**

DISILLUSIONMENT

Disillusionment is the dark side of illumination, or revelation. It happens when reality distorts our ideals. When encountering our self-imposed concepts and beliefs about What Is, we must be prepared to die and be reborn lest we end up eating the menu instead of the meal and lowering our overall Intelligence with each passing moment. If our preconceptions are out-of-sync with what's happening, then we ignore the truth and continue living a lie **or** release our attachment to ego and start living for **what is most true.** Sometimes, there's suffering involved depending on how much we resist letting go. The revelation occurs when you are able to answer the following question: ***What are you living for?***

ON BEING LOVED

Often times ritual work (as described in this book) is not always personally and socially "validating" or affirming, as it emphasizes Source Relations. People may never have the opportunity to get to know each other socially. The format of this medium is set up to bypass personal interaction in favor of supporting an "interplay of forces". It is important for those who plan to work at length in this medium to have either an active social life outside the Lab and/or somebody to go home to and be loved by. In this way, we are able to meet our personal needs first before entering the Rare Area. Otherwise, various forms of "neediness" tend to arise and take up group time which could be spent gathering momentum for exploring Source Relations. If followed, the guidelines to this medium will introduce an alternative form for human interaction that transcends Encounter Group, Psycho-Drama, Psychotherapy formats and the like. These have their place, of course, yet there's another intention here: HOW DO RITUALS WORK ? WHAT AM I LIVING FOR ? WHY AM I HERE ? WHO ARE YOU ?! WHEN DO WE BEGIN ?

TREMBLING AND SHAKING

Due to this medium's propensity to trigger living realities, the body may feel like *trembling and shaking* at times. When an energetic acceleration is occuring, it is up to us to make it easy on ourselves. Certain physiological adjustments help to clear the way: **breathing, jerking, twitching, yelling, whimpering, trembling, shaking, etc.** These occur when we release the grip on ourselves...our bodies. When things get real intense, **stay loose.** This is all you have to remember. Your body will do the rest for you. Trembling and shaking are common during rapturous conversion points wherein the organism's vitality kicks into action and your body just wants to express itself directly without censorship, inhibition or judgement from the more moralistic/conceptual areas of your brain.

EXHAUSTION

Often, in the initial training period and when we break into new levels of work, a certain exhaustion can accompany us. This exhaustion serves a specific funciton in that it's a sign that we have more or less gotten past "the nonsense" and are now **ready to work...**that is, we are more receptive to being *transported and moved* by forces evoked. Usually this kind of exhaustion joins us right before the final, culminating ritual where some of us might rather just fall asleep or quit. This, of course, would be the worst time to do so due to the nature of what follows...***the regenerative powers of the second wind..*** This stuff tends to work best*without trying*.. It depends on your willingness to put your exhaustion **to work** so that you become open and receptive to being **carried by the forces evoked.**

PLAYING

A certain kind of "playing" is perhaps the most advanced form of ritual. It is characterized by a willingness to be completely subjected to the forces evoked while simultaneously selecting **not to identify with them.** Instead, there is a realization that we are **not** that which passes through us (no matter how powerful, ecstatic, or brilliant it is) but simply instruments for **its** expression. When the ego is not as involved, it is more free to play. A fierce kind of innocence replaces the more "adult" tendencies of irrevocable self-absorbtion and the all-too-serious business of (cough)... "the Work." Too much reverence ends up not being that reverent at all. ***True sophistication results from penetrating the core of human experience, thus releasing the innate innocence contained therein.***

RESISTANCES

Ritual excites resistance and awareness of same. I think it does this because it's set up to clarify our fundamental self-definitions and resistances are one way we define ourselves. It seems the primary dilemma of resistance is **resisting it.** This is why the ritual function of sanctifying resistance is useful. Sometimes, it's possible just to drop it. Other times, you kind of weasel around it but more often than not, you have to go right into its heart of darkness and work to break through to the other side. Resistance comes in many shades of grey: fear, distrust, suspicion, boredom, despair, judgment, frustration, anger, irritation, numbness, rapid-fire thinking, guilt, inertia, rebellion, talking, tension, expectations, spacing out, indolence, laziness, etc, etc...perhaps the most direct way to go is just recognizing them when they come up so you have a choice in the matter as to how you wish to respond.

AUTONOMY

There's an anarchistic element to this work as it challenges and fortifies participants' autonomy or, willingness to govern themselves. Autonomy develops as more aspects of Self are accepted, integrated and put to work. The degree of ones autonomy determines the degree by which one may tolerate autonomy in others. If everybody governed themselves, the function of an outside governing body would turn obsolete and a new kind of group order/gestalt/culture could sprout. To the degree we are autonomous is also the degree we may permit the existence of autonomous forces, that is to say...those with lives of their own, not subject to our control or cohersion..and not necessarily confined to a human body. Autonomy is a function of our singular being and is reflective of our Essence. Autonomy, is nothing to strive for in itself unless you're ready to explore its dark or, hidden side...immobilization, paralysis and crucifixion. **Rituals challenging our capacity to permit uncertainty feed our autonomy.**

INTELLIGENCE

One way I've seen Intelligence operate is through polarizations. A "third point" comes up, reflecting an awareness unidentified with either side of the polarity. This "third point" occurs as you move between polarities enough times to ask the question, "Who is it that is moving between the two sides of myself?" "Who am I?" Anything uniting opposition while transporting us beyond duality is Intelligent to me. I think polarizations even increase our Intelligence and help us become receptive to its purpose. What is the purpose of Intelligence? I think it is to generate more Intelligence, don't you ?.

RELAXATION

When the body is relaxed, it is receptive and thus more available to be moved by the forces and aspects of Self evoked in ritual. Without relaxation, you will tend to exhaust yourself. The most basic form of physical discipline is in **the ability to relax your body at will.** The training proceeds by minimizing arbitrary tension: **those not immediately required to execute the activity at hand.** While standing in NO-FORM, just use those muscles which stop you from falling down and relax everything else so the stance expresses rest and relaxation. Apply this to Sitting, Walking, Speaking,Laying Down, Etc.

When the body is in a state of wakeful relaxation, the signals traversir from the brain via the spinal axis to the muscles are received and processe more rapidly. Another advantage to this kind of repose is in its acceptan of multiple shifts of the body's center of gravity...from its concentration the chest to the pelvic region and, in rare instances, the shifting of on center of gravity **into the Earth** a few feet below the body itself! One fact supporting this kind of shift is emphasizing "down" and "settling" overall kinetic commands, especially with jumps and leaps. When jumpi up, focus on the ground and the downward motion and, let the leapi upward take care of itself. **To get solid, get down.**

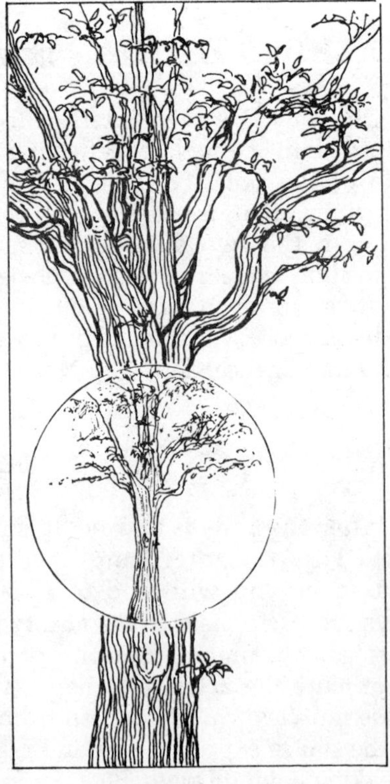

Guests of Honor

R. feather Anderson on **GEOMANCY**
FUTURE MEMORY *with Jose Arguelles*
Julian Simeon on **WILDERNESS**
STALKING THE DANCE *with Elizabeth Cogburn*
Kevin A. Lewis on **CONSTRUCTING A TEMPLE**
UNDOING YOURSELF *with Christopher S. Hyatt*

DITCH
BANK
NORTH MOUND
DITCH
Y HOLES
AUBREY HOLES
DITCH

GEOMANCY

Divining the Earth's Spirit

by Richard feather Anderson

Since the beginning of human society, people have sought out the right place to pitch camp, the right time to hunt or plant seeds, the purest most dependable source of water...as well as the places where healings occur, where visions are received and where contact with the Creator is facilitated. Until recently, human beings have always paid a great deal of attention to their relationship with the Earth. Before urbanization and industrialization, each family, tribe and/or village depended directly on the surrounding land to provide for their basic needs. Finding the most auspiscious time and place for each human activity and living in harmony with the natural world were so vitally important that each culture developed a set of principles and practices for maintaining its survival and prosperity. Ritual was a key element in these practices, for it centers us in the time-space continuum.

This body of knowledge is generally known as **geomancy,** or the Art of Harmonious Placement. Its practice has been used for locating the right place to dwell, come together as a community, commune with the Creator and bury and honor the ancestors. Each culture around the world developed its own flavor of geomancy in direct response to the geography and ecology of its region. There are certain underlying principles common to the various cultural forms of geomancy as all groups of people were responding to the same entity: Mother Earth, who develops certain universal patterns of growth or "laws" of nature. (I prefer to describe these as **patterns** rather than laws, since humans make laws, whereas nature abides by patterns.)

Geomancy can be best described as an ancient, holistic integrated system of natural philosophy and science once used to keep all human activity in harmony with natural patterns...from seasonal cycles to the universal proportions found in the way all organisms grow. Within the geomantic worldview, the Earth is seen as a conscious living entity,*the seat of divinity,* comprising both matter and spirit. The word geomancy literally means to "divine the Earth Spirit", or the energies and rhythms of a living Earth being. Geomancy's primary purpose is to maintain the web of life and keep the Earth Spirit alive and vital. This is done by overseeing the harmonious placement of cities, buildings and human activities. The megalithic circles and stone rows of northwestern Europe, for example, are thought to function as "acupuncture needles" for the planet. (Just as acupuncture is used to stimulate the flow of **ch'i** through our bodies, so too have geomantic practices maintained the flow of ch'i in the Earth's body).

Geomancy can be thought of as the **mother ritual -- the primal rite of centering and orienting ourselves** within our environment , for it has been our basic way of establishing our relationship with the land and all forms of life for countless thousands of years. It has to do with placing ourselves physically and psychologically within ever-expanding circles of relationship -- with the place we call home--with the people, animals, and plants with whom we share the land and -- with the cycles of the weather and the seasons. And so, our predacessors sited every structure with regard for the flowing veins of energy within the Earth's body, so as not to sever Her arteries, and devised elaborate accurate calendars to ride the waves of the Earth's cycles.

The first ritual of geomancy is to establish the center and boundaries of a settlement, and to recognize the natural boundaries of the region and/or watershed we inhabit. By declaring a center and periphery, a community's sense of place is created. (Indeed, at the root of all ritual practice are activities which center and orient us within our world and connect us with the Universal Consciousness of the Creator.) It is rather uncanny to realize that most of the ritual forms worldwide include ***movement in a cross pattern-- connecting us to the four cardinal directions, all that is above our heads and below our feet and, a reference to the center and circumference of the ritual place or Holy ground.***

Looking for the origins of these patterns brings up many questions: Why is it that most of our ancient cities have been constructed within circular walls interrupted by gate towers in the four directions ? Why are so many nation's capitols situated on their eastern coasts ? Why does the English word **orientation** mean "to face the rising sun ?" The answers to these and similar questions about archetypal symbols and ritual patterns lie in the principles and practices of geomancy.

BASIC PRINCIPLES OF GEOMANCY

The Earth Spirit that geomancy seeks to define was represented in ancient cultures by a dragon or serpent. In China, this practice of divination is called **feng-shui,** which means "wind and water", referring to the Chinese saying that the Earth Spirit is as incomprehensible as the wind and as ungraspable as the water. The breath of the Dragon is the Life Force of the Earth, which includes the blustering wind and the billowing clouds as well as the biomagnetic currents running in veins through the body of the Earth like the acupuncture meridians refered to earlier.

Associated with dragons and serpents in cross cultural mythologies is a magic pearl or egg, which legends say is created in the womb of the dragon. The pearl represents the Moon, the tides, weather and emotional cycles.

Cultures that practice geomancy consider the Earth to be **a living, conscious, sacred being... the creatrix and provider of all life.** The land is named after their primary Earth Mother figure as a constant reminder of its sacredness. Asia, Africa and Europe are goddess-named continents. Eire, Scotia and Turtle Island are the native and mythically-based names of Ireland, Scotland, and North America. The Gaia Hypothesis, neo-shamanism, Goddess spirituality and the bioregional and Green Movements are currently reviving this sense of the sacred and sentient nature of the Earth.

The Indo-European tribes that spread over India, the Mideast, the Mediterranean, Africa and Europe carry the idea a step further in their institution of **sacred kingship.** The sacred king was not a ruler with executive powers. He was, instead, responsible for maintaining the tribe's harmonious relationship with the land. **As such, he was ritually married to the land... to the Earth Mother.** The Arthurian legends are probably the most familiar example of sacred kingship. Arthur was responsible for maintaining the balance of nature and the fertility of the land by channeling the life force between Heaven and Earth. He was the figure who ritually stood at the center of the four provinces, the womb or Holy Grail of the sacred landscape, and distributed all material wealth equally and justly and resolved conflicts without bloodshed. If he failed to fulfill these functions, he was removed by elders, priests or matriarchs but never dispatched by violent means. (Spilling his blood was as taboo as cutting the breast of the Earth Mother to whom he was united). To become geomancers and earth stewards today, become like the sacred kings, marry the land and follow the ancient Arthurian mandate that, "You and the land are one."

A SENSE OF PLACE

To reiterate, the most basic way to create a sense of place is to establish the center and boundaries of the community. In geomantic traditions, a physical/spiritual center could be established in many ways: by setting up an omphalos stone, a labyrinth, a sacred tree or precinct, a village green or marketplace. Boundaries were created by city walls and gates, a "no man's land", green belts, or the recognition of a sacred landscape incorporating the surrounding mountains and rivers. During the Roman Empire, whenever they established a camp, fortification or town, they divined a center, then scribed the boundaries. They enacted a ritual called "cutting the first furrow" by plowing around the boundaries three times, sunwise. When they came to each of the four quarters, they would lift the plow and **not sever the breast of the Earth at that point.**

Socially, to become a community, ie., to create "common-unity", everyone needs to agree on the focus and purpose (center) as well as the extent or limits (boundaries) of their common activities. Many a cooperative business or intentional New Age community has wrestled with unresolvable conflicts born of an unwillingness to set limits or reject people for membership who do not agree with its fundamental principles. Lack of a well-defined center or boundaries can lead to the feeling that there is "no there, there", as with suburbia, the commercial "strip" and other forms of urban sprawl. Creating a clearly identifiable edge for a settlement also functions to contain the industrious energy of its inhabitants, preventing its dissipation across the landscape. This is similar to "casting the circle" in the preparation stage of a ritual -- a procedure which contains the shared energy of the celebrants, permitting its magnification.

A SENSE OF TIME

Until very recently, a culture's sense of time was linked with the agricultural year and the cycles of the Moon, the Sun, and the Stars. Buildings and temples were oriented to function as Astrological Calendars. Some of the megalithic stone circles of Europe were constructed with their geometrical axes (they are egg-shaped) oriented to the points on the horizon that mark the rising and the setting of the sun and the moon at midsummer and midwinter solstices at approximately **NE, NW, SE, and SW, depending on latitude.** Using these precise observatories, vast numbers of physically separated people could coordinate their celebrations to utilize the power collective consciousness has when simultaneously focused towards a singular purpose. Chinese villages, Indian pueblos, Etc., were oriented to the Four Directions with windows admitting light across central plazas at the solstices, so the group was dwelling figuratively within the wheel of the year. All of these Earth-centered cultures developed complex mythologies and ritual dramas describing the Earth's cycles, functioning to place themselves emotionally and psychologically in time and space.

SITING OF BUILDINGS

Greek, Roman, Egyptian temples and Gothic Cathedrals were sited to incorporate a sense of center, boundaries, landscape, the four directions and passage of sacred time. The foundation stones were set at a time auspiscious to the deity or patron saint (represented by a particular star or planet visible or on the horizon at that time), which in turn represented the archetypal forces necessary for the function that building was to serve. An East-West axis would be generated from the morning and evening sun's shadow projected from a central pole onto the perimeter of the building site. This created a perceptual as well as more accurate East-West axis than possible with a compass, since the magnetic poles shift so frequently. The shape and proportions of the building also related to its function (e.g., pyramidal granaries whose shape actually helps preserve the seeds.)

All of these ancient structures on sacred sites were built according to sacred geometry, a system of proportions based on universal ratios found in the growth patterns of all organisms and in the harmonic intervals of the musical scale. These "Golden Proportions" are illustrated in Leonardo da Vinci's famous drawing of the man proscribing a circle and square. I think the ancient builders knew how to use the Golden Mean to shape any enclosure to resonate with a particular frequency which facilitated a chosen activity. According to some researchers, the echos in Gothic cathedrals resonate at the same frequency **(Seven & A Half Hz)** as the Earth, quartz crystals, and the human brain while in a deeply relaxed, meditative "alpha" state. As a result, these temples create a vibration that attunes us with the Earth both physiologically and spiritually.

Resonant spaces can also put a community of people in tune with each other. Group singing or chanting in an acoustically alive place is a powerful way to achieve a sense of common unity. When any group makes vowel sounds together in free-form fashion, without a leader or script, the group sound will eventually reach a single pitch or chord. The same phenomena occurs with pendulums or grandfather clocks -- at first they swing randomly, but within 24 hours they will have synchronized themselves. So when we participate in community soundings, we are attuning ourselves with our neighbors.

To live in harmony with the Earth, we need to develop a modern fo of geomancy and learn to apply its principles to industrial as wel agricultural contexts, combining appropriate technologies with intuitive sense of what is in harmony with the natural history and patte of a particular site. We will need to integrate and remember the comr roots of the disciplines of architecture, ecology, geology, astrono astrology, sacred geometry, music, dance, and ritual into a new geoma cosmology.

Richard feather Anderson

is the founding director of the Westcoast Institute of Sacred Ecolog Berkeley, California, where he teaches geomancy and shamanism. Trai as an architect, with extensive experience in yoga, ecology, astrology, mythology, he currently researches megalithic structures and power sp in Europe and North America. He is also a well-known leader in Radical Faerie Goddess community and travels extensively sharing geomantic knowledge. For info, write: 2816 Ninth St., Berkeley CA 947

Stonehenge (Dr. Charleton's perspective, 1663)

FUTURE MEMORY

An Interview with Jose Arguelles, Ph.D.

By Antero Alli

JOSE ARGUELLES is author of Transformative Vision, Earth Ascending and The Mayan Factor, as well as co-director of Planet Art Network. When not living with his family in Boulder,Colorado, Jose travels extensively throughout the Americas initiating "resonant core groups" and other activities coinciding with his ongoing research. A poet, musician, painter and art historian...Arguelles is completely commited to communicating his visions of Planetary Intelligence and its inter-galactic correspondences. This interview took place at his home on the 22nd of September, 1986, right after he improvided a melody on his shakuhachi bamboo flute which he brings everywhere to initiate ceremonies at hand...

Antero Alli: How would you describe the process of resonance?

Jose Arguelles: To me, resonance is being completely melted into the situation and getting to a place where there's no barriers between what you think you are and what the situation is. One of the ways to melt the barrier and enhance the already existing resonance is through music. Mostly I play the Shakuhachi...a Japanese bamboo flute. After a certain tuning period, there's a total flow and melting into the situation. This is what I mean by by going into the resonance and even amplifying it.

AA: The Earth feeds us. How do humans, according to your view, go about feeding the earth? How do we make it reciprocal?

JA: That's a good way of putting it. I think the way we make it reciprocal is going back to what I was talking about and that's melting the barriers. Right now, we're in a "mental house or framework" that views your question as being outlandish. That point of view, as you know, is a brief historical abberation. For the most part, there have been many different kinds of people in most traditional cultures have held some kind of view that it is not just the Earth that feeds us that we give back to the Earth. I think the way we give back to the Earth and feed it is through cultivating profound states of receptivity...where we're first of all able to listen and really hear the resonances and vibrations coming to us and nurturing ourselves with those so that we might give back through what I'll call right harmonic action. This could take all sorts of different forms...from creating a rock garden to playing the flute on a cliffside to conducting a ritual ceremony that attunes a whole group of people to a particular rhythmic pulsation of the Earth's process. The particular view I have of who we are as human beings is that basically we are bio-electromagnetic batteries and the Earth is a geo-electromagnetic battery and... the Sun is a solar electromagnetic battery. So, when I talk about opening up and operating on the same circuit, that's how we feed the Earth. When we attune ourselves properly, we open up to that whole continuum. The feeding occurs through understanding and regulating your circuit properly and to create a resonance between your circuit and the terrestrial and solar circuits, so that you have a matching of electromagnetic frequencies. That's what keeps the whole system going...not only the Earth but the Sun.

AA: Describe your personal vision of geomancy and its relation to people on the planet at this time period.

JA: Setting up resonances with the three circuits I mentioned creates a unified circuit. Now, in terms of geomancy, what that means is locating places on the planet (most of them known by traditional peoples here and there) that seem to be particularly active in terms of their geo-electromagnetic energy and the idea there is to re-activate these places with attuned human bio-electromagnetic batteries. This is a reciprocal activation. What I've been working towards over the past several years is a highly practical form of geomancy to occur August 16 & 17 1987, where 144,000 human beings functioning as bio-electromagnetic batteries to be positioned at as many of the key sacred places on the planet as possible...synchronized at one moment beginning at dawn of August 16, 1987. This event is refered to as Harmonic Convergence. Through a totally open receptive attunement to the Earth conducted by 144,000 humans who are functioning as a synchronized and unified bio-electromagnetic battery...and tuning into the geo-electromagnetic battery, you're going to get a particular kind of electrical discharge. This discharge goes out and amps the total field. This is the idea.

AA: Speak about your ideas of the function of quartz crystals in their relation to this work.

JA: It's clear that in the last few years quartz crystals have become pretty popular and myself am no exception. My coming into quartz crystals was highly intuitive and was sparked by my encounter with Dyani Iwahoo who, when meeting my wife and I, remarked that our minds are very similar and we should be working with crystals. My work with crystals is to co-precipitate information or what's been called "channeling". What I've found is that crystals induce is a mild state of synesthesia or euphoria and ecstasy. This state, which is really quite cellular, simultaneously opens up nodes of information and imagery. These later will be discursively translated into metaphors or useful information links in the work that I'm doing. I find, at least for myself, it's like having a kind of cosmic walkie-talkie that's helpful in facilitating analogical leaps. The relation of crystals to geomancy...when you're talking about crystals, you're talking in some way about the primary vibrational structure in the universe...the hexagonal structural shape, a six-sided one, underlying cellular formation. What we call matter is built up of crystalline form, so **the Earth itself is a crystal.** The core vibrational structure at the center of the Earth is crystalline in nature. We're talking about a vibrational structure and not a literal crystal at the center of the Earth. *(Editors Note: Soon after this interview, there was scientific evidence announced to the effect that the Earth's core was, indeed, crystalline in nature.)* Plato, who got his knowledge from what was left over from Egyptian wisdom, knew that the Earth had a geometrical crystalline type of structure. The Earth itself, then, functions as a mega-crystal and obviously the use of quartz crystals becomes very handy in creating a field of attunement with the Earth. One possibility is doing crystal plantings for enhancing this kind of attunement. I think this has to be done very carefully. One needs to understand the location, what's nearby and the intent involved.

AA: Can you describe the process of locating a place and the appropriate manner of planting crystals?

JA: As far as the appropriateness of place, generally we're talking about them there hills...wilderness and near wilderness. You have to move very slowly and be aware of ridges, rivers and so forth to feel out where the right place might be. The only reason to do it is to create a field of attunement, really, with the Earth and to send a message to the Earth that there are certain members of the human community acting on behalf of the whole who are responsive to the needs of the Earth at this time. I think that's the proper attitude. The instructions I've received for crystal planting have to do with creating a circle and planting six no-more-than-one-pound size quartz crystals in the form of a six-pointed star, which is inscribed by a hexagon. At the center, an amethyst...the seventh crystal which refers to the seventh or violet ray. This is, in a way, ceremonial magick. It's another reason why this has to be done with a lot of careful consideration and respect...impure motives create adverse reactions, in other words. The reciprocal purpose of the people doing it is to increase their own bonding and kinship with the Earth. That's what is keeping us here and evolving us.

AA: So this is a ceremony where people plant crystals in this formation and stand around it to become receptive to the Earth's signal and respondwith a message back to the Earth,.. so the circle is a conduit for reciprocal communication.

JA: That's right.

AA: You've been studying Mayan civilization and their calendric systems. What do they have to say about living on the Earth at this time?

JA: Pretty much every thing I've told you. It has nothing to do with becoming in resonance, really. I call what I'm doing a neo-Mayan science and the basis of that is the development of a resonant field paradigm. Resonance and electromagnetism are primary. Matter is a secondary derivative or epi-phenomena of these two. When you begin to consider this perspective, you'll see it's the reverse of the prevailing scientific system. The psychic and social implications of this resonant field paradigm are quite enormous as they lead us to a lifestyle of terrestrial resonance and a technology based on a matching of psychic/solar frequencies. The sun is operating through what we might call a galactic program which is generated from the core of the galaxy...what the Mayans called Hunab Ku. This core emits the master program that is mediated by the different stars to the differing planetary systems. Our sun is then, continuously emiting sets of patterns which are simultaneously energy and information. These can be synthesized down to the readings of the binary sunspot cycles. Certain numerical patterns are determined by these sunspot cycles...23 year cycles...11-1/2 year cycles...and these are all accomodated by the Mayan matrix, the 260-unit Tzolkin calendar or mental pattern.

AA: What are some of the other "earth prophecies" you've encountered in your work and in meeting people?

JA: One way to envision the Harmonic Convergence dates of August 16 & 17 of 1987 is like a vortex reaching its apex, or point, and then it opens out again. This way, you have a particular kind of energy that goes to that point there and a whole other kind of energy happening after passing through it. As the vortex opens out, it starts another cycle where we enter a condition where we'll be experiencing a mental re-polarization. We've been dominated by particular mental fields since the 17th century (The Age of Reason) and what we'll be seeing is that this mental field is going to be reversed. In Mayan terms, it's the 13th baktun which began in 1618 when

Decarte published his meditations and kicked the whole thing off. The work I've been doing and that you're doing and others are doing is gettting ready to set in place a knowledge frame to be the foundations for the new mental house being built as this vortex starts over again. August 16 & 17 initiates this transition. By the summer of 1992, the resistance of the collapsing old mental house will pretty much come to an end. At this point, we enter another 20-year phase...the very last twenty years of the entire Mayan Great Cycle, which began in 3113 BC. In this last twenty-year cycle, once we've got the old machine stopped we'll witness on the one hand the final full flowering of the species we call Homo Sapiens. We're just about done, we've done all we could. We've come up against our stupidity and brilliance, so we're going to be given the opportunity to relax and let a final flowering occur. By 2012 AD, when the cycle closes out, that's when we shift to evolutionary patterns and that's when we get commpletely interfaced with what I call the galactic federation.

AA: Terrence McKenna uses that same year, 2012, doesn't he?

JA: Yeah.

AA: How would you characterize this new mental house we're shifting into during this polarization you're refering to?

JA: One of the terms that's around now is the new solar age which is definitely a reattunement to the sun in all respects. What I envision there'll be in the transition period is a shift from the "myth of progress" to the splendor of synchronicity and the reality of nowness. People are going to experience a much greater expansion of what we nowadays call "psychic abilities". There will be a critical point around 2007, in those last five years, where there'll be a return of the most primary, aboriginal kind of sense of "what do we really need, anyways, to really be happy and alive?" On the other hand, due to the accumulated 25,000 years of human experience, there'll be an incredible knowledge and sense of wisdom. It'll be a real Golden Age at that time and an understanding of the link up with the other six star systems of this portion of the galactic federation. For those who are receptive, there will be a slight disorientation not unlike the deja vu experience. There will, in this loosening up phase, be a release of archetypal memory, genetic patterns...that haven't been activated yet or have been dormant a long time or both. A highly renewed inspiration will occur...

To contact Dr. Arguelles &/or Planet Art Network, write:
P.O. Box 6111, Boulder, CO 80306.

WILDERNESS : Ritual As Personal Response

by Julian Simeon

For an instant, I stood awestruck...my feet frozen in the sand. The moon was supposed to be full but there it was in the night sky, as if some devious gods had decided to choke the light out of it. I wanted to drop to my knees to pray. I was scared...scared beyond rational thought. What could I do to bring back the light of the full moon? Suddenly I realized I was witnessing a lunar eclipse.

I had gone to the beach that evening to build a fire, watch the full moon, and listen to the pounding of the surf. I had not known there would be a lunar eclipse. The experience leveled me. Humbled for that instant, the fear of God was placed in me. I thought we were all doomed. For one fleeting moment, I was the neolithic shaman wanting to cry out for the survival of myself, my tribe and my world. I have often thought about that moment and my immediate response to it. It was an unknowing, unprepared and unrehearsed reaction. It was my gut level response to the mystery of Nature.

It is this type of natural respose to wilderness that I wish to explore further. I feel these innate reactions are **the essence of ritual.** Wilderness excursions often evoke a humbling acknowedgement of the greater unknown. I am fascinated by the effect of wilderness upon us 20th century inhabitants of the Earth. Driving in cars, living in houses, shopping in supermarkets...limits our interaction with Nature. I find it increasingly difficult to feel peace and gratitude while surrounded by the chaos of city life. I get caught up in commuter traffic, grocery lines, media advertisements, nuclear fears, financial worries, job burnout and all the rest that comes along with 20th Century American life. Often my insecurities of who I am, what I am doing, and how I am doing it, influence the way I live my day to day life. My response to the overwhelming chaos of city life has been to retreat to the wilderness for solitude, reflection, and rejuvenation. I frame the wilderness experience as a **rite of passage,** a time out from inner city life allowing for these periods of reflection and regeneration. I find that the quality of group interactions occuring during wilderness experiences permit greater competency, self-esteem and overall trust in self and, others. All this has added up to the nurturance of hope.

So, what happens when we go to the wilderness? As a university student, I was fortunate enough to have found a program allowing me to do graduate work in Wilderness Psychology. Wilderness, defined hereafter, is any natural pristine environment relatively unscarred by the effects of civilization. These two-week trips would follow a simple format: ***No tents, no stoves, no sugar, no coffee, no tobacco, no drugs, no books, no cameras, no paper...no luxuries.***

We made a committment to look at our cultural addictions, our relationship to ourselves, each other and to the Earth. We operated on consensus, using the group circle as a collective structure . One consensus everybody agreed to was dropping our "city names". We were addressed as "man in khaki shorts," or "woman with brown wavy hair". This mode of labeling continued until individuals found a "wilderness name". Names varied from "Willow" to "Feather", "Maya", "Canyon Bull", "Blood of Hawk", "Twin Star", and "Raven". The idea was to have a name choose us. This simple game seems to help people leave their "city selves" behind, while allowing time to explore different aspects of their personality.

On one Spring trip we made to the slick red rock canyons of Southern Utah, the final group circle before entering the wilderness agreed to discuss our relationship ***with "accidents" and our fears of "the wilds."*** The notion of No Accidents was presented in the light that so-called "accidents" occur whenever we are not in touch with our needs. People tend to become "accident-prone" as ways of getting attention from others and to indirectly demand others to meet their needs for them. A pact was made to be in touch with our needs and to communicate them when possible, i.e., when somebody needs a hug or needs to talk. Discussing our fears helped relieve anxiety and sometimes dispel unnecessary illusions. The fears included everything from "taking a dump in the middle of the night" to the fear of hunters, snakes, and of the unknown, in general.

On the final night of one trip where I fullfilled the role of wilderness guide, I prepared **a fire circle**. Prior to lighting the fire, I verbally framed my intention to the group. I told them I felt the most difficult part of any wilderness journey was the return to civilization, where one is really challenged to integrate what has been learned. I refered to the fire as an *entity* that not only gives us light and warms the body but also, perhaps, feeds our spirit. I suggested that the group approach the fire as this nourishing entity by feeding it wood. Each piece of wood was consecrated as an **offering**. Each person was asked to make a prayer or wish with each piece of wood offered into the fire. Bathing in the light and warmth of the fire, people asked for strength to carry on in their daily lives. This simple ceremony seemed to have a profound effect upon the people present. It was a direct response to the wilderness environment and the reality of returning to the city.

On a different wilderness excursion where only men participated, the time came for everybody to go their own ways to explore a 3-day period of **alone time**. The sun set as I built a small fire to cook my evening meal. I watched two deer approach the beach to lick salt. As darkness settled in, my own fear of the dark gradually influenced my attention. I fed the fire increasingly larger pieces of wood (due to the vast abundance of drift and milled wood washed ashore from numerous, sunken pirate ships, I placed actual logs into the fire). I was alone on that beach. My fire was a huge inferno lighting up an area a hundred yards in each direction.

The fire eased my fear and soon, it became obvious I would vigil throughout the long night on the beach. While contemplating decisions which would effect my life for year to come, I made a prayer with each piece of wood offered to the blazing fire. Feeling around for wood, I found a piece which felt extremely good in my hands. Upon closer inspection, I saw what I was holding. It was man-made club, a weapon, perhaps from an old pirate that had broken bones...cracked skulls...or worse yet, killed a human being. Quickly, I placed the weapon aside too afraid to let my mind wander further into its possible history.

I looked into the fire asking, *"Why are there weapons?"* I sat in the sad silence thinking about my question. Slowly, memories from my adolescent years came back to me. I hung out with a street gang and we used to make clubs similar to the weapon I'd just found. I cried as my guilt surfaced full force. The violence and anger I so despised in others was within me. I asked forgiveness from every person I'd ever thought or called a nigger, whop, kike, chink, gook, spic, honky. I thought of every person I had intentionally or even unintentionally hurt, hit or verbally abused. I fed the fire more wood, crying out for forgiveness from all those people. As I sat to the west of the fire, I felt soothed by its warm light.

I then had the urge to move clockwise around the fire in order to sit in the east. My perspective was different from there. I found myself thinking about all the people who had ever hurt me in my life. I recalled the times I'd been oppressed, hit, abused, and made to feel worthless. I found it in my heart to forgive each and every one of them; whether I knew them or not, I forgave them. I felt something moving deep within my soul. Instinctively, I moved around the fire and sat down on the south side . As I stared at the light, I found the strength to forgive myself for all the reasons of my guilt. My mood began to lift, as if the smoke and light from the fire were cleansing me. I felt lightened and peaceful within. I moved around the fire again and sat in the north. In silence, I forgave God for for having let me experience all the suffering in my life and, at the same time, asked God's forgiveness for all my shortcomings. A cycle was completed. I prayed for strength to become non-violent. I prayed as I disarmed, world leaders would also disarm. It was a ritual emerging naturally from the environment, the fire and, myself.

Over the past several years, I've led a number of groups on wilderness trips...people from all walks of life. I have discovered an ongoing bias in my approach to "wilderness work". First, I believe that the Earth is alive. Not only do I believe it is alive, but also that it is a highly intelligent and conscious being. I felt, in all circumstances, the wilderness to be the healer..the teacher...the guide. Secondly, I feel if we listen close enough, we can hear the Earth "speak" to us.

The wilderness works in many ways, on many levels. It is like a container of endless potential. On my wilderness journeys, I've been able to explore and transcend the polarities of Light and Dark, Good and Evil, Masculine and Feminine, Known and Unknown. However, I feel it takes awhile for it to have the deepest effect. Barring any "leveling experiences" like unexpected eclipses, I think it takes 2-3 days for the tapes in my mind to slow down so I could begin to fully appreciate the surroundings. As the journey continues, I've found it helps to accomplish various tasks. This gives the mind something to focus on while the wilderness quietly begins to work its "magic".

One night, while camped on the Middle Fork of the Eel River, I was tending the fire for an all-night ceremony. The moon was full that evening. I was out with a group of 16 men and women from the university and these were the final days in a two-week trip. As I got up to get some wood from the stack we'd collected, There was a strange sensation in my hand. The wood I held in my arms seemed to come to life. I looked at them closely and was enthralled by the lines and grain in the wood. Intuitively, I felt the time and energy it took to create those dried pieces of wood. At one time they were alive but now, in my arms, they felt like ***ancient elders...like the sacred bones of my ancestors*** and I ritually danced to the fire with them, reverently placing them inside the growing flames. I felt the "sacred bones" burn and transform into heat, light and smoke and that whatever information they contained was being transmitted to those ready to receive it.

Later that night, as I sang and played the drum, something came to me. It was so simple and clear. It felt like a message from the earth. All at once I knew, "The Earth needs to hear our songs". I responded with a song that brought tears to my eyes. I felt incredibly blessed. Again, my response was one of complete gratitude and joy in celebration of life. Time after time, the wilderness has allowed me to appreciate the very simple things of life. I think that this acknowledgement is **the *crux* of ritual.**

I like to think of the wilderness an a metaphor for the human unconscious with all its potential. When I'm out there alone, there is no running or hiding...there is no pretending. I'm faced with myself and Nature. The many times I've worked through my fears and guilt have always led me to a greater appreciation of life. This "working through" are my own personal rituals, rituals following no structure or beliefs but my own. I find the wilderness to be an incredible help in evoking such rituals. I believe the wilderness has the potential to ignite deep instinctual memories of a time when we lived more attuned to the earth's energies. This evocation reminds us of our simple, sacred relationship to the earth. As I stated earlier, I feel the hardest task of any wilderness excursion is in the return to civilization. We are challenged to implement what we have learned.

The return to civilization is like re-entering a "waking slumber"... a state where we are awake to our daily routines but asleep to the simple truths of living. It's as if we forget that we have forgotten the sacredness and interconnectedness of all living things. I feel our task is to wake up from this slumber, remember what has been forgotten, then...engage in a life inspired to live in gratitude and humility. Perhaps in doing so, we can save our planet for the children of our children's children.

JULIAN SIMEON

is an educator and counselor in the field of human services. He organizes and leads wilderness excursions for those interested in coinciding personal growth with planetary harmony.

For more info, write:

JULIAN SIMEON at 4160 Balfour Avenue, Oakland CA 94610

STALKING THE DANCE

An Interview with Elizabeth Cogburn

by Antero Alli

ELIZABETH COGBURN is a Shamanic Qabalist who travels around the world setting up sacred ceremonies that have developed, over the past twenty years, from the exploration of generic ritual forms and patterns. Working with people from all walks of life, Elizabeth's total commitment to forging the very old with the very new has given birth to an entire ritual technology drawing from both traditional and contemporary foundations. This interview took place September 25th 1986, while she had some time to discuss her work between ceremonies she was conducting on the East Coast of the United States.

ANTERO ALLI: How have you arrived at what you're doing now ?

ELIZABETH COGBURN: For twenty years, I've been exploring the creation of sacred ceremonial with the intention of establishing it as a valid art form and a way of spiritual expression in contemporary American life. We began with a large drum and a circle of dancers. Over the years, we've evolved a basic form -- a dance mandala -- within which we improvise the sound field, the dance and the dramas of our soul's Becoming. This process and their forms have proven themselves sufficiently **generic** to the human condition that I've been able to bring completely inexperienced groups to the point of holding together the sound and the dance all night long or towards all day dances. We've coined the name **Long Dances** for these. This training has often been accomplished in less than 24 hours. I also like the term "ceremonial" as it includes many rituals throughout the multiple levels of human endeavor while simultaneously engaging various levels of intensity. For me, a mere "routine" becomes a **ritual** when it is done with conscious awareness and intention. **A ritual turns sacred when this conscious intention is carried out with reverence, devotion and service to a Higher Power for the greater good of All Life -- *not just for personal gratification.***

Eventually, we felt a real need to become much more explicit about "the story" we are living by which our ceremonials, in some sense, re-enact. It had become clear to us that this is the great tradition of sacred ceremonial as transformational technology everywhere throughout all time among humans. These ceremonials are, in some way, the re-enactments of the stories (theories, cosmologies, myths) **that people live by.** All of us are spinning out the stories we're living by all the time...mostly, unconsciously. As we began to delve into the stories the New Song members were living by, we discovered many of us were students in the western, non-Jewish tradition of the Qabalah and, were in fact, members of the same training program in the same Temple. This story of who and what we are, where we came from, how we got here, why we are here and what happens to us when we "die"...all fits in with our inner sense of Truth. So, in 1984, we declared that all New Song Ceremonials would hence forth take place on the Qabalistic Tree of Life and that the Qabalah would comprise our map and method of spiritual discipline and unfoldment.

AA: Describe the prepatory rites involved in setting up these ceremonies...

EC: When I accept an invitation to create a Long Dance, I am in meditation seeking Guidance about that Dance. The intensity of the meditation increases as the date approaches. **You could say I am tracking, stalking and hunting that Dance...I am courting it and cultivating its energy field.** I'm considering the season, the zodiacal period, the corresponding Paths on theTree of Life, the planetary location, the constellation of people sponsoring the Dance and... what I hear from them regarding their central concerns and their stages of development. I am listening to and watching what is going on in the world...what the outer story indicates about what may be stirring in our Collective Subconscious. As I meditate, I walk the Tree of Life or its surrounding Medicine Wheel as they are laid out in the garden of the New Song Home lodge, where...directions and designs for that Dance come to me. I record and elaborate them in my design book. Later, when I have arrived at the place of the Dance and am in council with its co-creating sponsors, elements of these designs are then woven into our loose score for the Dance.

Another preparation I've done for many years is "Elizabeth's Letter to the Co-Hearts of the Dance." This is mailed to all our participants well ahead of our meeting. It contains meditations on the Paths of the Tree corresponding to this feast, along with other images, thoughts and special concerns with which I would like people to seed their minds. This initiates many levels of bonding to take hold by the time our eyes and hands meet in the first circle of the ceremonial. These are written anew for every Dance, no matter how many years we have been keeping that particular feast. If we are living in the moment, which is the real practice of the Qabalah, every time is always the first time for THAT Dance.

AA: As a ritual catalyst, what are some tools you might share with others ?

EC: The universe is made of sound. Words are instruments of power. **To name is to create.** To create living ritual -- that which has the power to effect lasting transformations within the participants -- there must be competent and inspired leadership fully honored and supported by all present. This alliance generates something like an electro-magnetic field drawing in, circulating and drawing out the power of the Spirit. Everyone can then direct this energy within themselves according to their own level of skill, understanding and maturity. This encourages and dignifies development of the highest possible levels of skillful leadership in all members of the circle according to their special lights and talents which empower the rituals and the lives of all who partake in them.

AA: What are some of the occupational hazards of your work...you know, the dangers of ritual-making ?

EC: There are traps along the way that we do well to be aware of. **Inflation** is one of them -- leaders getting "shot up" with themselves by personally identifying with the power moving through them in the ritual workings. I think this rooted in the immature and erroneous assumption that there is such a thing as "personal power" or that we humans are the source of the power that moves through us or...that to "be empowered" is to have power over someone else. One avoids or outgrows this trap by **learning to identify with the Higher Self** rather than the personal ego through realizing, **in ones bones,** that there is only One Power and that we are *ALL centers of expression for this Source.* We become increasingly accessible to this Power as we acknowledge Its true Source and refine our personalities...our egos...to be humble and ever more effective servants of the One Power that creates, sustains and transforms all Life.

A measure of ones development in this regard is the ease with which one can provide responsible, skillful leadership when appropriate and co-operate with the same when that is appropriate. **This is the power-from-within, power with, win/win game essential to living ritual, a humane sustainable culture and a vital creative process of Peace on Earth.**

Perhaps the companion/contrast to inflation would be **trivialization.** I notice a great hunger and eagerness for meaningful rutual and ceremony as I travel around my circuit. As the "closet ritualists" emerge and congregate, there can be a tendency to underestimate the energies that are being invoked in serious ritual and the Skill & Training required to Read &

Handle these energy fields. What is essential to the craft of a ritualist is to **know how to "call in" or "bring down" the right powers...to know how to contain, direct and release the energy that is generated.** Eager potential ritual leaders who develop some forms and collect nice paraphenalia and who proceed to perform rituals **before** they have done their inner "homework" of refining their own physical personalities (egos)...before learning how to recognize and handle energy fields...well, they're likely to find themselves in the position of the sorcerer's apprentice -- generating chaos.

Another aspect of this trivialization I see is the lack of distinction between rituals which are really effecting transformations in the lives and psyches of the practitioners and...those which merely produce a pleasant, happy emotional glow. The latter are valid and necessary but to confuse them with the deeper process suggests unnecessary limits on the field of possibilities for the soul's growth.

AA: How do you go about containing the forces evoked during ceremony ?

EC: **Our ceremonials are theaters for the soul.** As such, we seek to provide a safe and expansive context in which people can explore and share their inner worlds...designing and effecting such changes in their ways of being in the world as they may choose. **We are also courting ecstacy as a state of consciousness beyond concept.** We recognize a common human need for ecstatic experience ranking with our needs for food, drink, elimination and sleep and...**where this need is not honored and provided for in "right-hand paths", *it will always erupt in violence.*** We say that our Dances are prayers. We pray by dancing, singing and drumming **in pictures -- *meaning that we cultivate and hold the images of the changes we are seeking as we create our ceremonials.*** To commit to the Dance, is to offer a Give-away of yourself, body and soul, to the well being of the Greater Life. So we say, "make your dance a give-away, not a throw-away." **Ecstacy does not imply frenzy; gross motor activity is not synonomous with high energy.**

There is a great deal of spontaneous improvisation of sound field, dance and drama within our form but this does not mean license -- it must be ***appropriate spontaneity.*** That is, it must **fit the Whole.** You must be aware of what is going on around you and how what you are doing fits with the Whole. It is expected that you will go no further "out" in your inner worlds than you can find your way back, without hurting or endangering others in the corporate spirit of the Dance. **We are courting bliss with awareness.** This disciplining of consciousness is both rigorous and joyful.

AA: Are there fixed roles or positions participants play during the enactment of these ecstatic rites that support containment ?

EC: We have positions at various stages of skill. We have **Soul Watchers** on duty on the Dance Ground at all times.They are trained to "see" what is going on with each person on the Dance Ground at all times. They are there to help people find their way "out" and back again, if need be and, to see that the energy on the Ground does not get "out of hand." That is where maturity, understanding and skill are tested. **I believe that a good Soul Watcher will be someone who has faced and made some rite of passage with their own death and, their own insanity.** People who have not undergone such initiations tend to project their own fears on the dancers and misinterpret situations by placing too narrow a limit on the experience of others or by allowing delicate moments to careen into chaos. We want to permit the widest, deepest, most varied range of experience possible this side of chaos. Skill, in this aspect of containment, grows with the experience and continuity of the group.

The Soul Watcher has a partner during the dance called *The Outrider,* whose task is protecting the circle from intrusion from the outside. Where there is Light, there must also be Shadow. Moths are attracted to flame. We've had bikers, drunks, riflemen, police, and the idle curious...to fires, floods, blizzards, wind storms and torrential rains descend upon us during Dances. **One rule states that unless you're Outriding or Soul Watching, *you dance,* no matter what, unless you are called to assist.** I cannot say enough praise of the people I have danced with over the years with respect to their ability to handle every challenge that has come to us from either the outside or the inside. In 20 years, we've had no accidents and no serious illness of either mind or body. So, we feel encouraged that we are on the right track and have guidelines for helping us take on whatever challenge is served up and, that we may have information to share that might be helpful to others.

Another position I will add to this discussion of containment is that of the **Shaman.** "Holding the hoop" for the Dances I lead, I am on duty and available all the time to both the Outriders and Soul Watchers. In addition, I am reading many levels or dimensions of the energy field at once while frequently initiating adjustments to enhance and contain the ground. When the Sufis trained me to drum for their zikr dances, they taught me that the job of the drummer is to sit in the midst of the dance and (with the drum) **ground the energy while sending everybody to heaven.** That is good instruction for leaders of rituals.

AA: Where does "the void" of NO-FORM come into play ?

EC: (laughing): Oh, my goodness...what a mouthful! (more laughing). As a Qabalist, I take "the void" to mean the ground of being from whence we came...of which are a manifestation and to which we shall return. It's beyond name, form and gender, time, space and description. We open our dances with a spiral coiling in around the center which we understand to represent the Aleph Point, the No-Point, the Void...where all old patterns dissolve and new ones seeded. In a sense, the whole Dance happens in the void. Since we are willing to entertain the possibility of "voiding" ourselves, we're able in ways unnameable to particpate in this Mystery and then... return from the Dance through the same spiral...renewed, changed and made Whole.

AA: Are you refering to "ego-death" ?

EC: **In Qabalah, we do not seek the death of the ego.** Our task is in educating and strengthening the personal ego to its proper function as a humble servant and administrative assistant to the Higher Self. The ego is there to mediate between the inner, deep knowings of the Soul -- that which is "Above" -- and the immediate conditions and transactions of daily life on Earth -- that which is "Below." People with weak egos can't carry their own weight in the world. They are not good survivors or thrivors. They tend to be unfocused, ineffectual, ungrounded airy-fairy bliss ninnies. On the other hand, we have the tyrannical overbearing ego of the adolescent hero who always dies of hubris -- of taking upon itself glory belonging to the gods. Rather than refering to the death of that ego, I'd rather think in terms of transforming all of that good energy into an ego that has learned that it is not the source of itself but a servant of the One Source. Then, the ego recognizes it has no power of its own yet can be a fine center of expression for the One Power that knows that truth of the saying, "of myself I do nothing"...but through the One Doer, the Higher Self...

AA: ...the ego becomes devotional...

EC: Yes, yes...very much so...

ELIZABETH COGBURN

can be contacted by writing: c/o The New Song Ceremonial House
6741 Edgewood NW, Albuquerque, NEW MEXICO 87107

ON CONSTRUCTING A TEMPLE...

by Kevin A. Lewis

Anyone who has been involved with kinetic spirituality (as opposed to gathering dust in a church) long enough to see the benefits will also find themselves up against the problem of how to anchor it, i.e., to make it something more than an idea they carry around under their hat. This has been a common need to all forms of ritual (religious and/or spiritual) throughout history. How do we make it Real? So, thousands of places have come about around the world where some aspect of the multi-varied astral universe intersects with the material plane through human effort. Cromlechs, pyramids, mounds, cathedrals...all fall under the heading of Temples. As doorways to Somewhere Else, Temples are visible reminders that you can't get There from here but you can from **Here in the Temple** and that is what we shall attempt to find out hereafter.

Individually, this translates into the fact that the only Sacred Spot that is completely workable is the one that most closely replicates the inner wiring of the mind interacting with it. Or, to re-coin an old phrase, if you want the Temple to work right, build it yourself... This is an ideal approach for several reasons: 1) An individual Temple requires little physical effort and expense, as 65% of it exists on the astral plane (i.e., the imagination). 2) One is free to appropriate "materials" (thought-forms, psychic memory imprints, etc.) from existing Temples to add to the structure of ones own. 3) An individual Temple, if carefully built and maintained, gives a much higher return on a spiritual investment than most operating public Temples and, provided you don't speculate in Bad Energy, you Temple will bypass the often ruinous karma taxes that so many investors in the Public Vibrations Fund have to deal with.

All these considerations notwithstanding, building and maintaining a Temple involves considerable sustained effort at first (as does anything worth having) thus, the process of creating one may be one of the most thoroughgoing spiritual exercises around. This might be expected, for in the final stages of development, an individual Temple (whether at home or outdoors) is nothing less than a "secret passage to the Universe..."

There are 3 basic ground designs for most Temples in the world. It is these that we'll draw on to form the foundation of private individual construction. They are: **Pyramidal, Circular,** and **Cruciform**. (Bear in mind, of course, that these don't necessarily apply to Tellurian Temples...those natural power regions such as canyons, caverns, mountains, and forests. These places are shaped by Forces that are a power and purpose unto Themselves. Later, we'll investigate a method for detecting these...)

All three Temple designs have on thing in common: Four Directions. To settle down into the nuts-and-bolts process of Temple construction, we will start out with the Pyramidal layout. Taking a compass, mark the four directions as they apply to your room, garage, backyard or wherever you are. The thing we wish to know is whether the four walls of your room more or less line up with the four directions. (If the *corners* of the room align with the four directions, see the Cruciform or Circular floor plans). The four directions coincide with the Four Elements as such: **AIR -- East, FIRE -- South, WATER -- West, and EARTH -- North.** In each of the areas you have marked, place in a clockwise motion the following or similar items: AIR -- East: A Tibetan Bell or wind chime. FIRE -- South: A red candle. WATER -- West: A chalice of water. EARTH -- North: A potted plant or a rock or a dish of salt. (When taking your Temple apart, remove the items counter-clockwise, starting from EARTH) The four elements are symbolized in the Traditional Tarot as the Aces of the Minor Arcana from which you can extract further information. In the Tarot, you will also discover (albeit somewhat hidden) most of the surviving basic Temple blueprints of centuries past.

There are a lot of things to add to this humble beginning but first let us briefly touch upon the other two Temple designs. A Cruciform Temple may be seen in any of the great medieval cathedrals of Europe and England, as well as the ziggurats of primordial Mesopotamia. If the four corners of your room align with the four directions, then the center of your space will be seen as the central point of intersection of the four great lines of Elemental current running through the Earth, forming a great equilateral cross marked out by massive pillars, tornadoes, waterfalls, or volcanoes...whatever appeals to the imaginative faculties. However far out we may eventually take our design, it is best to study layouts of a few actual existing temples for ideas at the beginning.

A couple of fertile ideas for the design of Circular Temples can be drawn from Stonehenge, as well as some of the great Taoist and Buddhist structures in China. Besides the cornerstones dedicated to the forces of the four elements, our Temple will need certain equipment; things we might call "psionic amplifiers" or, if that sounds odd, "aids to the imagination". One of the main items is a point of focus, i.e., **an altar.** The altar functions as a sort of spiritual workbench. Candles will be necessary as a Power switch: When the candles are lit, the Temple is **"on"...**when the candles are out, the Temple is **"off".** Any sort of small exotic table will do as an altar, although a dresser or chest carries the advantage of storage space. The altar should be placed in whichever direction your Temple is drawing its "current" from; most altars face East and the rising sun, or North and the magnetic pole. However, **all directions are sacred** at various times, so the more your altar is rotatable, the better.

Aside from candles, an altar requires a symbol of wholeness...not unlike a central image in a church. This represents the particular aspect of the Universe our Temple plugs into. The color of the candles, perhaps, could correspond with our Intention in the rituals enacted in the Temple. The more the items on the altar are related in intent, the greater their capacity to infuse cohesion into our point of focus. They are all united in their capacity to bring us closer to the Being/Reality appealed to. It will also be easily seen how the various New Age/Positive Thinking toys such as Affirmation, Crystals, etc. work much better in a charged Temple atmosphere than merely an ordinary living or bedroom.

Now, since the very idea of a Temple presupposes the notion of cosmological Intelligence, or constancy, it is appropriate that the operation and construction of one contain factors relating these ideas to the internal workings. For example, most Eastern religions schedule their major activities according to the phases of the Moon (as did the Old Testament Hebrews), specifically the New and Full Moons. As far as the Western public religions are concerned, this has fallen out of practice because practitioners are taught to not expect anything "real" to occur from these efforts and so, nothing does.

Our private Temples might, at least, operate according to the idea that the "tides of the Astral Sea" are on the rise from the New to the Full Moon and thus best for outgoing activities like water-skiing and raquetball. From the Full Moon to the New Moon (the waning phase), on the other hand, is more appropriate for inward reflection and meditative activities. If we were to decide on inviting the influence of other planets into our Temple, we will need to surround ourselves with items reminding us of those planets, and the Forces they represent. Having covered most of the salient points of Temple building -- and the many unfilled details and fine points to be colored in by yourselves -- we will touch briefly upon a few tips for effective Temple operation.

We mentioned four elements. There is a fifth, **Spirit** or *aether*, which is found in the **capstone** of the Temple. The capstone is a charged area located at **the convergence point of all four directions/elements and is located directly above the center of the Temple...above the head, usually several feet or more.** It is charged with an originating, creative intent...a point in space from which the four elements and directions not only converge but spring forth from. Our personal relationship with this potential state is the basis for our capacity for charging the capstone. Without such a relationship, it would be somewhat futile to construct a

Temple in the first place. Simply an awareness of this coordinate is enough to proffer the necessary perspective during ritual enactment to refer what we are doing back to its Source. Like the Source itself, there would be no real Temple without the capstone.

Most, if not all, private Temples ultimately draw much of their Power by linking up with various Temple Groupminds around the globe; the idea being that a private Temple is much better equipped to screen out most of the superstitious fear and psychic pollution the public Temples become riddled with. As anyone who reads the newspapers or history books is aware, there were and are Temple Groupminds that are veritable compost heaps of astral garbage...the moral being, never worship anything that prefers blood over wine...

A few brief words on Tellurian Temples may be of use to those wishing to explore them. **A Tellurian Temple is any land-connected Elemental Vortex where the four Elements converge in a manner unusual or noticeably different from generally encountered levels of intensity.** Many of the major ones have been recognized in the form of being declared National Parks and the like. Other areas, which may only be a few feet in diameter, are only frequented by local spirits. Friendly Tellurian Temples (and not all of them are) may be a source of great rejuvenation, inspiration, and, **provided you only take what you're given**, materials for your own Temple use. This is the real thing and should be approached with the same care with which you would explore an unfamiliar, dark cave. Mechanics first: most Elemental Vortexes operate along the lines of what could be called a Triangle Power Concourse, or TPC. The TPC formula simply observes that in most areas of the Earth's surface, the proportions of the four Elements are divided along triadic lines -- three Elements manifest and one is "latent." Choosing an example at random, let's imagine ourselves in a mountainous region: high peaks, forested slopes, and a lake in the valley. Barring forest fires and volcanic eruptions, our operative Elements are obviously Earth-Air-Water with Fire being latent. If we stand on a mountain peak or ledge, the dominant Element is Air (which may blow us off the edge or its spaciousness cause a vertigo). Air, being an "active" element, would be placed on top of the Triangle to look like this:

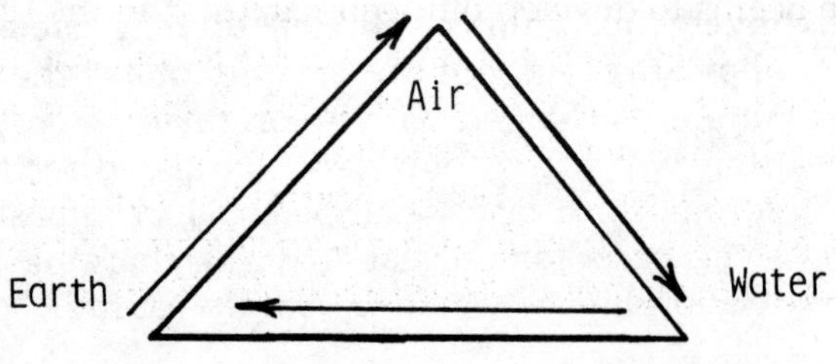

If we go swimming in the lake below, we'd have a "passive" Triangle. Other Triangles include:

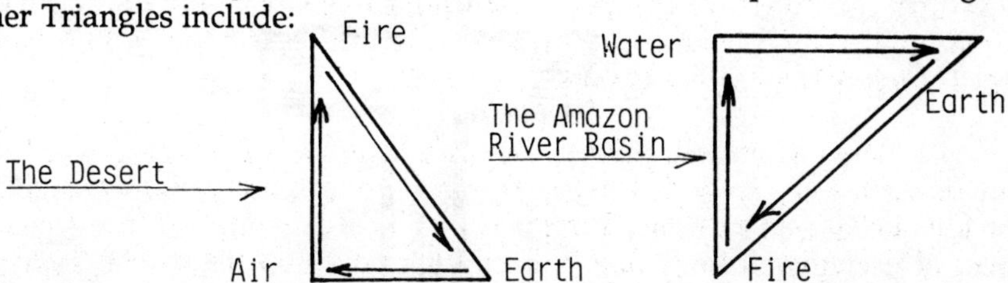

Using this as a loose guideline, we may gauge the approximate layout of Elemental surface areas we encounter. Caverns and large water surfaces, however, such as "Bermuda Triangles" and their like are often not Triangular but Biangular, increasing their intensity to the point of being dangerous to unwary visitors and the passerby (Elementals have to eat, too, y'know). Just treat theese regions with the same respect that you would a lot of high-velocity machinery with no safety bars. Spotting Tellurian Temples is a more or less subjective experience (some are no larger than a "fairy ring" of mushrooms under a tree) and so, we'll conclude by mentioning several of the more interesting...so, readers can explore for themselves.

1) **The Mayan Sacrificial Well at Chichen-Itza** is a natural sinkhole lake where the Mayans used to feed their people to the Undines. Very holy place but swimming is best done elsewhere.

2) **Mauna Loa National Park in Hawaii** is a good place to watch the periodic mating frenzy of Fire and Earth spirits. (Not a good area for condominium developers.)

3) **The Big Sur coastline along central California** is a very intense TPC of Water, Air,and Earth, and is best not taken lightly...especially around the Full and New moon.

4) **The Blue Hole of Belize is a Biangular Power Vortex off the coast of Central America** where divers report that after reaching the maximum safe depth, one begins to develop nitrogen narcosis; in the Blue Hole, this takes the form of an overwhelming urge to swim all the way to the bottom. (A steady succession of divers have yielded and are now happily reincarnated as dolphins out there...somewhere...)

Kevin A. Lewis is a writer and "Temple contractor" currently engaged in the practical side of Hermetic spirituality and magical research .

Inquiries may be addressed to: 815 Alice St. #B, Monterey, CA 93940

AGH! NO... IT CAN'T BE.. MY.. MY.. DOGMA.. IT'S.. IT'S.. OUTMODED! ARRRGH!! ARRRGH!!

UNDOING YOURSELF

An Interview with Christopher S. Hyatt, Ph.D

By Antero Alli

This interview commenced on October 31st, 1986, at the home of Dr. Hyatt, which is also administration office for the Golden Dawn Society and Temple, U.S.A. The actual location of this place, as well as Dr. Hyatt's identity are to remain concealed for now at his request; he granted this first interview under a pact of confidentiality. Mr. Hyatt's long-term discipleship and friendship with Golden Dawn Adept and chief spokesman, Israel Regardie, (who died March 10, 1985) contributed to his current status as director of the elitist circle of The Golden Dawn and President of the Golden Dawn Society and Temple. Without revealing his identity, Hyatt struck me as a rather dynamic, penetrating presence given to the sheer delight of articulating what is immediate and obvious yet often unspoken of. He seemed more Magus than Mystic and impressed me as one of the most gutsy, animated and outrageous libertarian sorts I've coincided with to date.

ANTERO ALLI: In sixty-six words or less, where did the Order of the Golden Dawn originate and from your point of view, what is its current status ?

CHRISTOPHER S. HYATT: Well, I really don't have any point of view about where it began. Historically, people wish to believe it began at the beginning of time. In terms of written information, it had its origins approximately in 1887 or 1888 in England through two gentlemen named Wescott and Mathers... and a few others... who claimed they had deciphered secret manuscripts obtained from a "secret lady" from Germany. Some people argue that this was a fact and others, that it is not. Dr. Israel Regardie solved the entire problem, in my opinion, by stating that it didn't really matter. What really mattered was the ethicacy of the techniques and that in the Golden Dawn, you had a complete system allowing the aspirant, through various meditations -- rituals -- exercises, to obtain (if you would) conversation with his Holy Guardian Angel. Or, in more modern terms via Jung... his Higher Self.

AA: What exactly is your function in the Golden Dawn since the death of Dr. Regardie ? What do you do ?

CSH: What Regardie wanted me to do was, if you would, to make sure to the best of my ability that the tradition of the Golden Dawn continue in both book form and, in temple form. You could say that I'm sort of an ambassador attempting to bridge the ancient qualities of the Golden Dawn with the modern interpretations and theories of current scientific research as it relates to conversation with the Higher Self. You see, each generation and society develops sets of language and theory relating best to the personal neural resonance of that set or, time period. The language of the Golden Dawn is quite archaic and many of us who do not have its historic sense in our own neural resonance find it difficult wading through the mass of ancient material... the Egyptian god-forms... Hebraic letters... the Enochiana and so forth. I firmly believe that this material needs to be brought to our current age in a new language.

AA: What kind of language ?

CSH: Well, much like you've done in your book, ANGEL TECH. You've taken a lot of ideas and brought them into the resonance of the people who are here on the planet right now. Another, perhaps more radical, example would be the task of updating the text of THE COMPLETE GOLDEN DAWN SYSTEM OF MAGIC to modern scientific terminology, which is something I'd love to see done. As young Alec said, "Our aim is religion and our method, science."

AA: The Golden Dawn seems to have gone underground after Crowley's reign. Do you forsee its emergence in the near future ?

CSH: There is, I think, a new emergence... at least for the time being. One reason for anything to be underground, as I see it, is due to the persecution resulting from the establishment of competing realities. The Golden Dawn was a competing reality to the many forms of Christianity present in England at that period. At that time the Golden Dawn was kept "secret" and rightly so. However, I'm very distrustful of secret societies because I think they're a form of self-aggrandizement whereby the people , individuals and leaders elevate themselves by keeping all the information to themselves. This tends to give a kind of mystique to the information when, in fact, there may be no validity to the information whatsoever. This is how deliberate mystification often leads to self-delusion. Keeping it secret proffers a mystique and a "validity" that may not actually be there. I think by presenting it openly and publically, for those people who are interested, we can discover the validity of any "secret system."

AA: According to your estimation, how many "official members" of the Golden Dawn are there at this time ?

CSH: It's very difficult to say. If we look at previous sales of Golden Dawn books and make lots of assumptions and a few fairly good inferences, I'd say probably thirty or forty thousand people. The Golden Dawn had a significant influence on the sub-culture of the Sixties and Seventies and has influenced many, many people... like... Alan Watts, Timothy Leary, Robert Anton Wilson and, numerous others. The Golden Dawn provided them with an alternative model from which to look into and down upon the numerous competing reality systems emerging in the Sixties and the Seventies. In a way, the Golden Dawn provided the foundation for a lot of the Mystical Movement that has taken place in this country's recent history.

AA: How did Robert Anton Wilson become a member of the Golden Dawn and how have his writings been influenced by its systems ?

CSH: Well... I think Bob is a member of all organizations and a member of no organization at all. I think he has been influenced by the writings of Aleister Crowley rather significantly and secondarily, the writings of Israel Regardie. Since both Crowley and Regardie were devotees of the Golden Dawn, their ambiance and attitudes have rubbed Bob in this way and then, that. This is especially true in Bob's ability to manipulate concepts and in his experimentations with ritual magic and the use of ones brain to influence events.

AA: From your perspective, what is the singular most vitalistic element in effective ritual without which, it would turn into an empty routine ?

CSH: I believe this requires a suitable aspirant and suitable initiators. We may view this in this simple way: the aspirant represents an energy and a color and the initiators represent an energy and color. When we perform a ritual, we mix all these energies and colors to create the desired effect... which is to elevate and enlighten the aspirant, as well as change the form and energy of the environment and the world we are all living in. Most rituals are rather empty, in that the people present are not capable of eliciting, containing, and projecting the appropriate energies and colors to create the necessary result... the required one.

AA: Will you speak more on the ritual function of "containment" and how it relates to keeping a ritual vital and alive ?

CSH: I think part of it has to do with being as empty as possible... in order that the proper energy or color, if you would, can be generated, expanded and manipulated to produce its desired effect. I think that most of us are just too full of things to be a proper container for the energy. This was the whole notion behind my so-called "outrageous" book, UNDOING YOURSELF, where I didn't have the restrictions placed on most authors by their publishers because... I am the publisher. Nor was I concerned about making money on the book. Therefore, I tried to present, through the printed media, the best way possible to "emptying oneself out." A spiritual laxative, if you will ...

AA: How important is the process of psychotherapy to involvement in the magickal systems of the Golden Dawn ?

CSH: I don't like the term "psychotherapy" anymore. You see, I used to be a licensed psychotherapist... officially sanctioned by the State because I had so much education and State-approved experience. As normally spoken of, I find psychotherapy a very restrictive, operative model. However, like Regardie, I have to agree that psychotherapy of one form or another is sort of essential before one enters into the world of "energy" expansion and containment. It gives one a certain perspective for differentiating specific major problems such as "wish fulfillment" from Real Work. I prefer the idea of a psycho-spiritual laxative rather than the word "psychotherapy" due to the idea of Emptying Out refered to earlier.

AA: How does the psychic function of "the shadow", as refered to by Jung, relate to your Psycho-Spiritual Laxative Theory ?

CSH: I think this is the major problematic issue all of us have been groping with who are engaged in the so-called "depth psychologies." Very few of us have the stomach, insight, and courage... and, the will... to make a Changing Whole out of ourselves. What we tend to do is reject, both consciously and automatically, those things which do not fit into our image of how we should be OR we reject those things we believe will increase the probabilities of rejection and/or punishment. So, in a sense, this Shadow is often more real than the Person because the Shadow becomes a depository where all the unwanted parts of ourselves are placed. It becomes a crystal, OK ? At the most inopportune times, we find our idealized images totally shattered by this much harder crystal. We have been taught, in this culture especially, to be hypocrites and self-deceivers. We have been given a model and told it is the ONLY reality and, that model happens to run contrary to our inherent potential and nature. We have become split... a split culture... schitzophrenic. The goal of man, at this level, is to become unified within himself so he may prepare for the next set of steps requiring individuals who can **contain** lots of energy, tension, and relaxation.

AA: How do you see The Shadow emergent in current society ?

CSH: I believe we're seeing it right now in the Fundamentalist movement, albeit, whether it's in science or religion, politics or the softer, correlative sciences...the so-called New Age movement, for example. What we see here is an attempt to repair a cracking egg. The only way fundamentalists' belief systems can cope with this is by digging their heels into the ground and forcing "objectivity, facts and knowledge" into opposing models by either ignoring them or... destroying those people representative of them. As a system is cracking, there is a growing tendency to enforce its dogma. These cracking systems are being forced to change by the Consciousness Movement and its interaction with High Tech.

You see, the human brain is wonderful in what it can do in terms of manipulating objects, creating all sorts of devices but it doesn't seem to do very well when it comes to more primitive aspects of its nature such as the Oral, Anal, and Sexual orientations via Freud or the first four circuits of Leary's grid and what you're doing in ANGEL TECH's first four grades. It is my opinion that these so-called "lower regions" are the real area requiring the most work and this is where I am staying... where I am stuck... where I am working.This is so the first four circuits can be brought up to match and integrate circuits five though eight, which are currently evolving.

AA: What are some of your visions regarding our future life on this planet ? And, if you recall, what were Regardie's ?

CSH: Regardie wasn't as "optimistic" as yourself and Bob Wilson. He agreed that, what Bob talked about in PROMETHEUS RISING and what you hinted at in the end of ANGEL TECH, would probably happen but not as quickly and easily as both you and Bob believe. I also agree with Regardie. I see that the Earth still requires some blood before it is ready to move onto new and different areas.

AA: Rather disconcerting, isn't it ? Will you elaborate ?

CSH: Yes, I will. I would like to be more popular... I'll say that first. My commitment to myself is to speak the truth as I experience it without considering sociological consequences. In other words, it's easy to sell tranquilizers and, sometimes we need tranquilizers. Speaking from the heart, I see that we are in an era of the Changing of the Guards. While analogy can be challenged, I'll choose to fall in that trap for now and believe that the Guards of the Ancient era...the one dying right now... are not willing to give up their authority so easily. I forsee, on a mass scale, that the New Age is not going to come into being as so many people believe and wish to believe. I see it as requiring a heck of a lot of blood, disruption, chaos, and pain for a mass change to occur. However, I do see small pockets able to live through this period without having to personally suffer the devastating effect of The Changing of the Guard.

AA: What are some of the deteriorating factors undermining social structures from societies such as the Golden Dawn to an entity as monumental as the United States government ?

CSH: I see it as a lack of flexibility. In other words, we have a model and try to make the world fit it, rather than going along with the data as it emerges. I published my GENERAL THEORY OF DISMANTLING awhile ago which stated that all of the so-called "structures" simply provided the illusion of Security... Pseudo-Security Syndrome, in other words. What society and culture err in is that they try and superimpose a solid structure on a fluid state. Everything changes, you see. And, they expect, after such an imposition, that everything will remain simply wonderful! Since everything is not simply wonderful, they paint illusions that it is and, that's called propaganda. Or, as Bob Wilson called it... **bovine excreta...** I simply call it bullshit while others call it worse, still. And THIS is the **murderer of man and all creativity...** this attempt to stifle us with pseudo-forms which are given Absolutist A Priori status, rather than relative a postiori status.

AA: Here, in the latter part of 20th Century America, do you see the role of ritual playing a significant part with the Common People ?

CSH: I do see a need for ritual of the sort which amplifies our current predicament and not just superimpose more pseudo-structures. This is why I created the UNDOING YOURSELF system. I firmly believe that you must **hollow out first...undo.** My idea is that we need to attack the fundamental regurgitations of people... those values and beliefs we haven't chosen but are simply "spouting." We need to work with those first and use ritual to do some of the hollowing out but even that has to be done with a person more interested in quality than quantity.

AA: What is Life After UNDOING YOURSELF like ?

CSH: After Undoing, one needs to rest. You give a jolt and you give some time. The process of Undoing Yourself is eternal. The crux and essence of it must be **functionally established and orchestrated properly.** Once that seed has been planted in the deepest part of a person's soul, the need for further orchestration and direction is minimal. Once you are undone and have had the first hollow space made for the seed to be put in, then it's a process of **integration.** Then, you undo some more... plant more seeds and integrate. Undoing... seeding...integration... and so forth.

AA: How would interested individuals go about studying material from the Golden Dawn System of Magic ?

CSH: They can write me at **FALCON PRESS, 2210 Wilshire Blvd., Suite 295, Santa Monica CA 90403** and request information on the Golden Dawn Correspondence Course. For those people who are ready to do more than that and have the means -- mentally, emotionally, financially and spiritually -- a number of us are always available to initiate the process of Undoing. That is to say, once you are loosened up enough, if you will, to have shaken loose from some of the dogma you've been wrapped up in.

bbell's
ENSED
UP
Camp
COND
SO
5
HIEROPHANT
ב

GLOSSARY

Brief Definitions of Ritual Terminology

altar -- a psionic amplifier; focal point in a Temple; spiritual workbench usually supporting a certain symbol of wholeness, i.e., cross, spiral, star

amplification -- intensifying enhancement of any given reality for clarifying the obvious and articulating its presence

archetypes -- powerful, numinous images illuminated and charged by autonomous psychic forces unseen in themselves yet expressed in dreams, mythologies, and ritual evocations

asocial -- any attitude bypassing social considerations and obligations for the purpose of setting up a Rare Area; shift from external to internal dependence; self-commitment necessary for ritual work.

attention -- necessary awareness for executing effective ritual; ability to incorporate and/or bypass interruptions towards a continuity of consciousness; degree of alertness

aura -- self as "energy field"; the particular quality present in your personal space at any given time; amplified as "body of light"

body of light -- those rituals affording the experience of internal illumination; capacity for absorbing, holding and transmitting light

boundarywork -- those tasks executed towards defining the periphery of the Little Circle and/or aura; the process of adjusting ones personal space to accomodate ones psychic/emotional territorial needs

breath -- connective current linking inner and outer space; self-reference device during times of personal crisis, i.e., "breathe..."

characterization -- advanced ritual theatre work; wherein a set of contact points converge to convey characteristics motivated by a purpose to tell a story and/or myth

charge -- the accumulative point of emotional and psychic condensation expressed positively as excitement and negatively as resistance; localized in a specific body area and/or throughout the entire system; the capacity for energizing a Rare Area, Little Circle and/or Ritual

cloud of unknowing -- internal device for setting up conditions conducive for magnetizing NO-FORM; bridge to potential state

commitment -- the Soul's degree of willingness to embodiment

contact point -- internal area of direct, intuitive merging with a particular quality, aspect, or force; source of stimulus inside the body and/or beyond the skin, in the aura itself

containment -- ritual device for minimizing dispersion usually involving an act of subjecting oneself to the influence of ones own emanations instead of releasing them outwardly and away from the self; see **boundarywork**

conversion -- a transition point wherein a state changes into another, i.e., the conversion from directing energy to serving it produces the resultant quality of a shift from one state into another; initiation;

dark rites -- rituals designed to elicit encounters with, expression of and integration in the Shadow function of the Self, primarily for the purpose of testing endurance and self-knowledge; evoking the vitalistic elements

design -- the patterns in a given quality, movement and/or state of being which, when detected, form the basis of choreography, movement and vocal forms emphasizing clarity of form

development -- the commitment necessary for following any given direction through to its conversion point and beyond to a new quality altogether; the result of self-commitment

directional -- motion predetermined by the personal will of the one moving; capacity for determining the precise outcome of movement by intending its speed, rhythm, style and tension levels; self-determined

dispersion -- any release of charge; talking is a "dispersion device" for discharging excess energy accumulated throughout ritual work; dispersion levels determine what kind of ritual is possible, as we can only absorb as much energy as we're able to contain; opposite of containment

economy -- advanced ritual theatre work emphasizing intentionality by minimizing arbitrary expression; distilling essences by playing it small; miniscule movements capable of conveying/containing strong forces

elements -- the autonomous forces of Earth, Water, Fire, Air, and Aether or Spirit; cornerstones of Temple construction; pieces to a ritual puzzle

form -- the clarity by which a given shape or quality gives of itself

four corners -- ritual device for constructing a Little Circle and/or Temple; each corner proffers distinct energetic service and function; device for containment and boundarywork

geomancy -- the artful science of divining earth energies; reading energy leylines, vortexes, and power spots for the purpose of understanding how to enter and operate with integrity in these areas; capacity for detecting planetary characteristics

gesture -- kinetic device for crystallizing the essence of a peak experience or energy level; a series of gestures form the basis of myth (see Myth)

grounding -- any process serving to stabilize current energy levels; overall connectedness to planet and gravity as a force; Earth-based activity

group circle -- ritual device for bringing a group together to discuss previous rituals, current intent and future possibilities; usually dedicated to non-judgmental feedback and direct reports of what actually happened, rather than philosophical speculations of what it all means

healing -- rituals quickening the innate; amplification of essence

idiosyncratic -- kinetic device for claiming ones own personal space; an ability for instilling a highly personal signature to ones vocal creations, movements and rituals; statement of uniqueness; incomparable

inflation -- condition of being self-identified wherein the ego is expanded and/or shrunk past its previous boundaries; the result of internal fusion between ego and Self; full of self (see DANGERS section)

initiation -- the result of those rituals triggering high degrees of uncertainty and creative response; transformative shift from one reality tunnel to another; conversion points

integrity -- the self-respect necessary for respecting others; a self-preservation device enabling endurance amidst great intensity;

intuition -- capacity for direct, open-ended contact with living forces; ability for tuning into a condition without imposing preconceptions, judgment and/or interpretation; first-hand knowledge

little circle -- that physical and psychic area dedicated to generating and containing presence throughout ritual preparations; personal space

magick -- personal contact with the Infinite; degree of comfort exhibited amidst uncertainty; the capacity for being at home in the unknown; those methodologies responsible for Initiation, Trance, and Transformation are "magickal systems"; synchronization of external and internal faculties and activities towards greater command over ones predicament

meditation -- first phase of the physical warm-up in ritual theatre; physical stillness in the position of your choice; coinciding ones attention with ones body in time and space; paying attention and listening

music -- psionic amplifier usually applied to enhance atmospheres and expressions of ritual participants and/or to influence their proceedings

myth -- an symbolic story animated by a series of charged moments; a sucession of gestures or tableaus bypassing cultural bias and founded in universality; a network of peak experiences arranged to convey thematic direction comprehended instantly by all who witness its unfolding

no-form -- void, nothingness, the potential state; in ritual, it can be approached through a rested standing position that initiates and resolves each ritual by its tendency to dissolve identification; a tool for discharging excess psychic energy or emotional investment; ego-deflation tactic; source of all forms; state of minimal expression

non-directional -- motion dictated by impulses, rhythms and pulses of the organism itself, usually after relaxing our grip on the body; organism's innate direction and force often realized through abandonment, exhaustion and surrender; innately determined

obstacle orientation -- the perspective enabling non-judgemental detection of resistances for their encounter, expression and release

pleasure -- motivating device for initiating the warm-up cycles, i.e., movement as pleasing, fun and nourishing; trance-dispersion device enabling a return to the five senses after more psychically-charged rituals

point of worship (POW) -- what one lives for; wherever ones Life revolves around, consciously or not; Source relations; place where identity is invested; ultimate values

polarizations -- ritual device for stabilizing emotional flexibility after the physical warm-up; physical and emotional oscillation between polar aspects producing greater energetic cohesion and balance

power spot -- that area on the floor or ground supportive of ones well being, usually detected by intuition; the basis of Little Circles (not to confused with a geomantic, energy vortex)

prayer -- internal dialogue and/or communion with Point of Worship; spiritual resonance; that physical position, gesture or ritual affording communication with the Diety Within; active ,passive, & silent prayer

preparation -- preliminary activities and adjustments for setting up a ritual(s), usually combining meditation, chanting, dancing and arranging of the physical location to accomodate the ritual intent; see sanctification

projection -- capacity for charging a chosen area for the purpose of activating a particular ritual; sending information and energy out of oneself and into another area, i.e., Little Circle for the purpose of entering that area to be subject to the projected influence.

psychic -- perceptive; the domain given to energetic operation as opposed to but not exclusive of physical and conceptual realities; capacity for extracting usable information from energetic contact; absence of projection

psychological -- symbolic interpretation of the psychic; the personal maps used to describe and refer to the living territories of our experience

quality -- the particular nature of a force

rare area -- space, as of yet, untouched by social projections, obligations and expectations; prerequisite condition for inviting spiritual presence; first task in setting up a ritual

resistance -- whatever is judged as not being OK the way it intrinsically is; frozen energy; source of immobility and self-definition; any impediment to direct flow of Life forces; inertia

resonator -- a kind of internal psychic chamber developed through the accumulation and assimilation of certain essential substances of ones being, the purpose of which is to excite empathy with Forces within and around us if we so choose;

rhythm -- kinetic, emotional and vocal device for expressing patterns of motion; method for stabilizing presence and continuity;

ritual -- the outcome of converging contact points in a particular setting after a specific preparation to do so; activities enhancing the awareness of human relationship with the living planetary entity; the intentional tasks executed to evoke a particular force for the purpose of its fulfillment

sacred -- holy (see Point of Worship); the sacrum; see sanctification

sacrifice -- to make sacred; the offering of something dear to oneself as an act of faith and a precursor for psychic discharge; psychic release

safety -- necessary condition for vulnerability

sanctification -- process of preparing a space for ritual through its consecration; heightening value of the element of space; self-empowerment; capacity for granting permission to be and for others to be; vocal creations, gestures and movement forms generated for the purpose of deepening and expanding thepresence of safety; benediction

scrupulous -- quality resultant from honoring the integrity and autonomy of ritual participants; necessary attitude for regarding others

setting -- the actual location a ritual is to take place

shock -- sudden disruption excited by an incongruity between personality and essence; usually resulting from an awareness of misalignment between images of Reality and Reality itself; a change occuring independent of ones volition; simultaneously, there's a disconnection with habitual response and an energetic acceleration; opportunity for self-rearrangement

social -- human function governing interpersonal relations, courtship, domestication, morality, collectivization, and group process in general

solitude -- gratifying element of being alone (all-one with oneself) usually a prerequisite to Source relations and exploring internal dependence

Source relations -- interactions exciting relationship between an individual and their source, or god; conversation with Higher Self or Guardian Angel

spinal flex -- second phase of physical warm-up in ritual theatre; dedicated to the gentle rendering of flexibility in the spinal column thus, activating the Central Nervous System (CNS) and neuromuscular responsiveness

spiritual -- that which is sensed; beyond words, categorization & thought

stretch -- third phase of physical warm-up in ritual theatre; dedicated to breathing into the muscles while they are stretching to become more malleable and receptive to the signals from the CNS

sweat -- fourth phase of the physical warm-up in ritual theatre; dedicated to generating enough heat to sweat; holy water

surrender -- total giving of self; necessary condition for development

talking -- psychological device for integrating emotional/psychic input often resulting from "deep work" and usually executed during the group circle; a bridge connecting the sacred to the social/conceptual for the purpose of exiting the ritual setting and entering the world outside; dispersion device

temple -- a physical and psychic process of constructing a charged and sanctified atmosphere conducive for evoking specific forces during ritual.

trance -- a primitive state of consciousness increasing ones sensitivity to illumination, sound, rhythm, visions, and play in general; (see Conversion, Initiation, Magick); gateway to the "body of light"

transitory run -- jogging forms designed to restore equillibrium between rituals (see Directional and Non-directional)

uncertainty -- condition permiting receptivity to new information; the capacity for confessing ignorance when one does not know; preliminary state to transformation; capacity for the idiosyncratic

vocal creations -- sonic resonance; those sounds produced by the direct expression of a particular contact point through the vocal instrument.

vulnerabilty -- necessary condition for surrender; dropping ones act; the strength implied in being oneself as one is

warm-up -- the preparatory cycles of meditation, spinal flex, stretch and sweat designed for the purpose of feeling the body deeply; necessary prerequisite to evoking archetypal forces; the act of becoming physically limber, malleable and mobile, stable and activated; ritual preparation

work -- any self-realizing activity synonymous with love

x (factor) -- a reference to the greater unknown; aspect of psyche which can never be completely known, described and/or figured out; the irrevocable mystery of our being; the delicious black hole centers of our spiritual origins

zen --

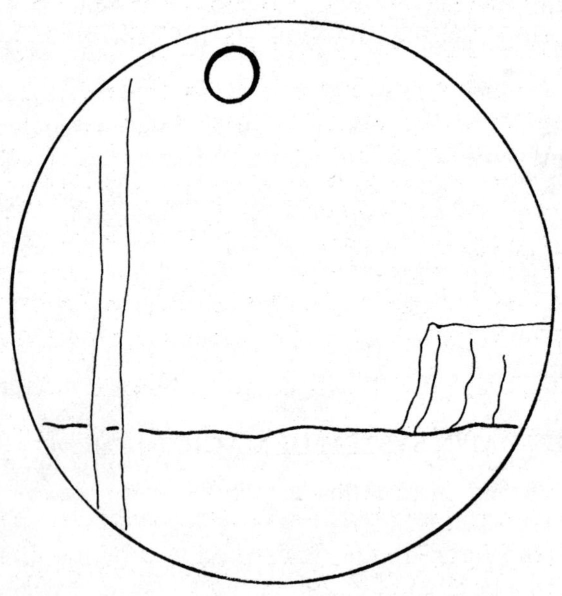

SUGGESTED READINGS

Geomancy:

SACRED GEOGRAPHY by Robert Lawlor...Thames & Hudson, London,
THE ANCIENT SCIENCE OF GEOMANCY by Nigel Pennick...Thames & Hudson, London, 1982
THE EARTH SPIRIT: ITS WAYS, SHRINES & MYSTERIES by John Mitchell...Thames & Hudson, London, 1982
FENG-SHUI: THE CHINESE ART OF PLACEMENT by SarahRossbach Dutton,NYC
SECRETS OF THE STONES by John Mitchell...Penguin Books, 1977

Temple Construction:

INCENSE: ITS RITUAL SIGNIFICANCE, USE & PREPARATION by Leo Vinci...Aquarian Press
CANDLE BURNING: ITS OCCULT SIGNIFICANCE by Michael Howard...Aquarian Press
THE NAME OF THE ROSE by Umberto Eco...Warner Books
CEREMONIAL MAGIC by Israel Regardie...Aquarian Press
THE COMPLETE GOLDEN DAWN SYSTEM OF MAGIC by Israel Regardie...Falcon Press (1,112 pgs, w. diagrams, illust., & instructions)

Ritual Preparation:

ENERGY, PRAYER AND RELAXATION by Israel Regardie...Falcon Press
UNDOING YOURSELF with Energized Meditations by Christopher S. Hyatt...Falcon Press, (re: SETTING UP A LAB)
ANGEL TECH: A Modern Shaman's Guide To Reality Selection by Antero Alli...Falcon Press, 1986 (re: CONSCIOUS EVOLUTION)
ZEN MIND, BEGINNER'S MIND by Shunryu Suzuki (re: NO-FORM)
PSYCHOLOGY OF THE TRANSFERENCE by Carl G. Jung...Princeton Press, 1954 (re: ALCHEMY)
THE COMPLETE GOLDEN DAWN SYSTEM OF MAGIC (see above)

Performance Ritual:

TOWARDS A POOR THEATRE by Jerzy Grotowski...Simon & Schuster
THE THEATRE AND ITS DOUBLE by Antonin Artaud

AFTERWORDS

This book has offered guidelines to a ritual technology capable of triggering internal forces for the overall purpose of being moved from within. A company of individuals disciplined in such an approach may wish to consider extending it into the public arena of **performance ritual.** If we are strong and vulnerable enough to be moved, certainly our presence is real enough to move others. This simple rule of thumb forms the kind of rapport necessary for evoking the miracle of a shared communion, or holiness, between audience and a performing company. It is, perhaps, the highest function and offering ritual can provide.

Ritual theatre can be experienced as an entire medium unto itself and/or a series of effective preparation rites for entering performance ceremonies, and/or a series of devices to enhance whatever ceremony seeks greater intergity. The techniques of ritual theatre have been, indeed, already utilized in theatre performance with much success. Many times ritual theatre would be woven into a patchwork design of Inter-Media performance rites with strands of music, poetry, dance, mime, method acting, ballet and visual effects included to complete the fabric. Such performances have been carried out by both professional and "naive" groups dedicated to preserving a strong ritualistic quality in the final product. The script material for these public performances have often developed from intensive pre-rehearsal sessions using this medium.

The shape and texture of ritual theatre has undergone many changes since its inception in 1976. Participating individuals tend to exude idiosyncratic and learned patterns of expression which have contributed to the overall shape of this medium. For example, dancers amplify the kinetic level while actors infuse psychological motives into the work. It's as if each individual cuts another facet on the crystal. It is in this way that every group is highly unique and each session, different from the rest.

Working with an ongoing group in this medium is the best way to find out what it's all about. For the beginning group, I suggest meeting no more than twice a week for several hours each time. This will more than suffice. After about three weeks of this (and if the warm-up and guidelines are followed correctly), everyone will know if this work is for them or not. Ritual theatre is not for everybody, by the way. However, for the right people (those who are able to continue working), the long-term results are well worth their while. And what are these? For me, three distinct qualities have emerged as a result of continuous work and they have all changed my life. One result of relating with **No-Form**, is that it's given me a certain perspective on myself. I mean, how can you take yourself too seriously when deep down you know you're just another *piece of the void?* The education of **self-commitment** has had an enormous impact on my willingness to integrate what I've learned into my own style of speaking, singing, walking, and moving. Finally, the **self-access** this work has excited has enabled me to listen to and tolerate the manifestations of others a little better by the virtue of my own deepening integrity.

The underlying principles of ritual theatre (especially No-Form, Contact Points, and Polarizations) have proven effective for breaking open the creative process in general. True artists already know there is no creation without intimacy with void. Somebody once told me that ***the gods favor emptiness*** and indeed creation comes through us when space has been made to serve its expression. We are, at best, **interpreters** rather than creators per se in that our task is translating spiritual signals or qualities into readable messages using the artistic conventions of our era, or making up our own. This is not always easy, especially for highly "creative types", myself notwithstanding. At times, we confuse ourselves with our so-called creations and perhaps do so to temporarily slow down the process with the inertia of our identifications. Those of us with less a need to become our creations bend towards the prolific, as the process of creation is eternal and never-ending.

Hopefully ritual theatre can amplify the ongoing dynamics within us so that our lives become more available to us. Maybe each day we can invite another piece of Earth inside and offer the planet a piece of ourselves. ***This alone can make all the difference in a world.*** Ritual is never separate from Life and ritual theatre, at best, is a lab for amplifying what's already happening so we can get a better handle on it. This has been the primary reason for setting aside a Rare Area ...to create an arbitrary division for getting a better look at ourselves. Sometimes, we have to pull ourselves apart to come together in new and more engaging ways than before. And this process is not always easy, as those who already know can attest. In closing, my hope has been to provide heuristic and actual data for enriching our working knowledge of ritual technology relatively unrestricted by the imposition of dogma, creed or religious doctrines. It seems we are entering an era wherein our capacity for containing vast amounts of light and knowledge is being challenged from all directions at once. Ritual knowledge, I believe, is instrumental for enduring the intensities at work and re-directing them to the light of day.

Antero Alli, Director
ParaTheatrical ReSearch PO Box 7513 Boulder CO 80306

About The Author

Born November 11, 1952 in Helsinki, Finland, Antero Alli has resided i the United States since May 23, 1962. Since then, he has emerged with 15-year background in the Performing Arts after having written, directec produced and acted in over a dozen original Inter-Media Theatre piece: Currently, he is director of ParaTheatrical Research, a core group o individuals dedicated to the development and practice of generic ritua forms as presented in *ALL RITES REVERSED.* Antero frequently tours th States presenting **Lectures and Workshops** from this material, as well a subject matter from his other book, ***ANGEL TECH:* A Modern Shaman' Guide To Reality Selection** (Falcon Press) and **The Angel Tec Correspondence Course (ATCC).**

Antero is an ordained Taoist priest and the recently appointec Temple (of Horus) Astrologer of the Order of the Golden Dawn, USA. I his spare time, he runs **ASTROLOGIK** (a Mail-Order Reading Service writes for various national magazines, and, on occasion, free-lance performance work. Upcoming projects include designing the forthcomin 21st Century Tarot, writing more books, doing more theatre an eventually joining forces with people who make movies. **Signed copies** c his books, *ANGEL TECH* and *ALL RITES REVERSED?!* are available b sending **$11. @ payable to the author, to the address below.** Inquirie regarding the ATCC, ASTROLOGIK, TOURS, BOOKS & TAPE and...Forthcoming Releases can also be addressed to:

ANTERO ALLI, Director
ParaTheatrical Research/Astrologik
P.O. BOX 7513 Boulder CO 80306
****